Praise for *Working Parents-to-be*

T0049435

From the 'real experts': current new parents and parents-to-be, most of whom I have never met but agreed to take a look and share their views...

As a first-time expectant parent venturing into the confusing and complex world of parental leave and return to work, this book was a game-changer. It is an essential read for anyone grappling with the complexities of this process, offering a wealth of invaluable tips and effective strategies.

The book breaks down each aspect of the journey into bite-sized chunks, providing a practical guide that you can refer to as needed. The exercises serve as an excellent tool for exploring personalised approaches, and my husband and I have already earmarked the weekday childcare plan and admin review for when our baby begins nursery next year!

What resonated with me the most is that while addressing the most common challenges encountered at each stage of this journey, the book also shines a light on the positive aspects. This newfound perspective has instilled in me a sense of confidence as I embark on this new chapter, allowing me to entertain the notion that parenthood could potentially enhance my performance at work, rather than assuming it will solely have a negative impact on my professional life.

Emma McKinley, Finance Director at Haleon plc in the UK & First time mum-to-be

I didn't think I needed help but Catherine's advice made a huge difference. I was offered sessions with Catherine through work. I thought I was on top of my return plans so was sceptical as to what I would gain but I'm so pleased I did. They helped me find my way back to some sense of normality in that period when everything feels like surviving. By the end I felt empowered and equipped to deal with the challenges. It also encouraged me to have conversations that meant not only me, but my partner and colleagues, were more informed, so everything was smoother and we all had more realistic expectations.

I found it both reassuring to confirm some things and enlightening to learn tips and ideas about things I hadn't thought about (one of which saved me from having a breakdown on my first day back because none of my clothes fitted!) It's brilliant to see this all packaged up in an easy-to-read book format – it is the next best thing to talking to Catherine and I would highly recommend it, you won't regret it.

Emma Griffiths, Planner at Brown & Co in the UK & First-time mum

As a gay dad in the US, returning to work following the birth of my second child was a daunting task. *Working Parents-to-be*, with its comprehensive ideas and practical templates, greatly simplified the overwhelming process of transitioning back to the workplace. I particularly appreciated Catherine's inclusive approach, which acknowledges the diverse family and work circumstances unique to each individual. The book offers indispensable tools for balancing professional responsibilities and parenting. It's an essential read for working parents, providing adaptable advice and celebrating each family's unique journey. I only wish I'd had it when I had my first child.

Alasdair Weddell, Senior Director at Peacock in the US & Dad on leave with second child

I absolutely loved this and finished it in less than 24 hours! How easy it is to pick up and put down. The reflections on what you'll learn and bring back to your career from becoming a parent. But my favourite element is the quotes which are not just from influential people. For me for example, a father talking about adoption and not knowing when they would need leave really resonated with me. And I think so much here will resonate for others. Thank you for putting this into a book.

Amanda Richardson, Technical Training Manager at National Gas in the UK & Adoptive mum-to-be

Thank you for creating this awesome guide – I feel a lot more prepared for maternity leave this second time around thanks to your book. I particularly valued the exercises to make me think about what's coming up and how it's prompted me to consider things I hadn't yet thought about – like contact while I'm on leave. It's made a real difference to how I approach conversations at work and how I feel about the transition.

Nichola, Strategy General Manager in Telco & Media, Sydney & Mum of toddler about to go on second maternity leave

I loved this! As someone who is currently on maternity leave but also who manages people, I wish I'd had this to refer to in the past. Many managers had their children a while ago and so it's really easy to make assumptions on what families are experiencing in today's world. This would be a great tool for them and, in fact, in my opinion it's a must-read!

Emma Munroe, Customer Vulnerability and Improvement Manager in Health Insurance, UK & Mum just starting second maternity leave

This guide reassured me, empowered me to seek help where it wasn't offered, to see the positive in shaping a new working dynamic that creates space to do better and ultimately to find and offer ally-ship through shared experiences in a pivotal and daunting life stage. For those newly juggling work and family life or anyone who manages people it provides a vital lifeline for a transitional period that's somewhat fallen through the gaps in the way of support.

Katherine Daly, Executive Director Client Services at Landor in Singapore & Mum-to-be

Catherine's personal insights make it feel like listening to a friend. It came just at the right time and motivated me to work out an informed return plan and think about how we organise life within our family – with two working parents. I especially loved that it offers advice throughout the different stages of becoming and being a working parent while trying to fill out the role of being the best parent to my child.

Aline, Head of Customer Experience at Sky, Germany & Mum currently on parental leave

Parenthood is a journey into the unknown, but that doesn't mean you need to leave everything to the universe. Catherine's book offers a pragmatic and universal guide with helpful tips and tricks for all soon-to-be working parents. It's easy to follow and gets to the point. I found it both reassuring that I was on the right track and insightful.

Tanja Crnogorac, Executive Strategy Director at Landor, Tokyo & Mum-to-be

We found this really helpful. It's such a challenge trying to find a good balance between life at home with an 8-month-old, and working part-time while sharing parental leave. With our little one starting daycare in a few months, using the tips and exercises in here have helped us make a solid plan, manage our expectations and feel more prepared for the transition!

Myrto Papageorgiou & Daniel Buschor, teachers in Sweden, job sharing & new parents currently sharing parental leave

This book talks to both the parent and the career person in you and I found the activity guides helped me to devise a simple, clear plan to make returning from parental leave feel far less daunting.

Trish Folan, General Manager at a Brand & Creative Agency in Australia & Mum on second (and last) maternity leave

And from people I admire for their work in this space and support of working parents

This is the book I really needed when I first became a working parent! Full of useful advice, it is a book to have by your side before, during and after parental leave. Buy it, keep it to hand, read it, and even write in it, using the frameworks and exercises to clarify your plans. It's well-structured, and with key takeaways set out at the end of each chapter, it is easy to read for busy working parents. Although our experiences may all be different, everyone will find something helpful in this book.

Kathryn Bishop CBE, Associate Fellow at Said Business School and author of *Board Talk and Make Your Own Map: Career Success Strategy for Women*

Catherine has created an excellent practical guide to working through the many challenges of becoming a working parent and it's great to see such valuable advice being made available to all.

Colin Jones, ex-COO, Sky

A super practical guide. What I really loved though is firstly the real-life examples of what being a working parent is all about… the good, the bad, and the ugly… secondly, that whilst the focus is naturally on the experience of the primary carer, Catherine also encourages readers to look at it from the perspective of others – notably partners and managers who play such a key role in the overall experience. Great seeing them included and getting some tips. And finally seeing examples of best practice sprinkled throughout to hopefully inspire us all as to what's possible.

Oliver Black, Former Managing Director of Bright Horizons, My Family Care and Tinies

A fantastic resource for new parents-to-be, with the self-reflective exercises particularly helpful to prompt the important discussions between partners and employers that are so rarely had. It's a toolkit very much for modern parents.

Han-Son Lee, Founder of DaddiLife – the leading content platform for dads and an HR consultancy for dads at work

Catherine and I have worked together for a number of years to provide group and 1-2-1 workplace coaching pre, during and post leave. Drawing on her own experience, she has always shared very realistic and practical advice. I'm delighted she has put pen to paper so these pearls of wisdom are accessible to an even wider audience, in a very structured way that makes it easy to dip in and out as you reach each stage and phase. The authentic everyday stories really bring the book to life and should make it very relatable to many on their joyful, yet challenging journey to becoming working parents.

Rachel Vecht, Founder and Director, Educating Matters

Not only is this a fantastic and much needed resource for all new or soon-to-be working parents, but I think this is a must read for managers and leaders who want to get a better insight into the challenges of working parenthood and how they can better support their teams through this critical time – getting it right can play a big role in improving the gender balance of an organisation.

Joy Burnford, Founder and CEO of Encompass Equality, gender balance champion and author of *Don't Fix Women*

A great read with lots of practical advice and guidance for working parents, this book also offers a valuable insight for leaders who are supporting parents.

Barry White, Head of Organisational Development, National Gas

It is wonderful to read such a clear, well written book, which includes both practical tips and helpful exercises throughout. It is incredibly inclusive and the way it is organised, with clear section summaries, also makes it very neurodivergent friendly. I know this book will be helpful to many and I have no hesitation in recommending it.

Dr Kara Davey, Clinical Psychologist and HR Consultant specialising in supporting new, expectant and bereaved parents in the UK

As a working mother of two, I wish this book had been available to me during a pivotal time in my life. The invaluable insights, practical advice and self-reflection exercises it offers would have been a beacon of guidance and reassurance to have had when I embarked on my journey back to the workforce. It's an indispensable companion for any parent navigating their leave and return to work after having children.

Jani Burwood, Head of People & Culture, Aurora Energy Research

We know from the work we do as a charity providing legal advice to parents and carers on their rights at work, there are many challenges during this crucial phase. It is daunting without proper guidance to help navigate the intricacies of parental leave so it's great to see a resource like this being made available to all working families. To help empower them to understand their options and how they might use them. And to guide them through essential conversations with employers, ensuring a return to work that is as seamless as possible.

Jane van Zyl, CEO Working Families

Working
Parents-to-be

Your guide to parental leave and return...

what to expect and how to make it work for you

CATHERINE OLIVER

First published in Great Britain by Practical Inspiration Publishing, 2024

ISBN 9781788605984 (hardback)
      9781788605991 (paperback)
      9781788606011 (epub)
      9781788606004 (mobi)

Want to bulk-buy copies of this book for your team and colleagues? We can customize the content and co-brand *Working Parents-to-be* to suit your business's needs.

Please email info@practicalinspiration.com for more details.

For Jo and Evie, my biggest supporters and my inspiration

And for all the new or soon-to-be working parents
out there – this is for you

Contents

Part 3: Returning to work

Preface

As a parent-to-be you will inevitably have a lot of questions. Many you'll find answers to at prenatal or adoption classes, which help you prepare for having a child and give you an opportunity to meet other parents-to-be in your area. But what about the questions you have as a working parent-to-be? To help you answer questions like 'How will I do my job as well as being a parent?', 'How do I approach a conversation around changing my working pattern?' or 'How do I create a return-to-work plan?'

The lucky few work for organizations who recognize this need and provide expert coaching to help them manage their leave and return. To help them make the transition to becoming a working parent. But what about everyone else? Most people are left to fend for themselves and count themselves lucky if their manager gets it.

This gap between the haves and the have nots has bugged me since early on in my years of supporting working parents. It has always struck me as unfair. And having supported many thousands of people who have chosen to take on the dual roles of parent and employee, I realized I was in a position to do something about it. So, if you're in the process of starting or adding to your family and you're intending to return to work (or at least considering it) – this book is for you.

And it's for you whether you're a first-time mum or a second-time dad. Whether you have a partner or are flying solo. Whether you are genetically related to your child or not. It is not a book about parenting. It is a book about how to manage your relationship with work when you take a period of leave to become a parent. Or you want to support someone close to you who is.

Why me? What's my story? When I had my daughter in 2011, I had a relatively good experience. I had a supportive manager and team. I worked for the UK broadcaster Sky at the time and, following the trend of large corporates, they had recently introduced enhanced benefits for parents, including six months on full pay, which I was able to benefit from, so I felt very much looked after. All of this didn't alter the fact that, at this point, I was the only member of my team with a young child. After about nine months back in the workplace I started to feel something was missing. That more could be done.

I remember vividly standing in front of the bathroom mirror one morning. My daughter was getting upset about me leaving (one of the first times) and it hit me that the challenges would be different, but they would always be there. Part of me is ashamed to admit it, as it seems so obvious, but during that period of my life I think I was very much surviving day to day. I was convinced I would get the hang of it, get everything organized and it would get easier. And of course, for anyone panicking, it does get easier, but that moment of shock, the realization the challenges would just change, was really important for me. It made me think hard about what I wanted – and that was to be able to talk to others who were going through the same experience as me.

The friends I had made through prenatal classes – via the National Childcare Trust (NCT) in the UK – had been a real lifeline while

I was on maternity leave, but were no longer filling that need. They returned to work at different times – some to much smaller organizations and others to large corporates like Sky, but none were at Sky. And every organization has its own unique culture. I wanted to share my experiences – the good, the bad and the ugly – with other parents who worked at Sky.

My personal reaction was to try to set up a network for working parents at Sky. To help those, like me, connect with others going through the same thing. At first, I thought I'd had a moment of genius coming up with the idea, but I quickly learned other organizations had these so called 'employee networks', just not Sky. Not yet anyway.

It took me some time to build the traction and get engagement, but nine months later, in the summer of 2013, Parents@Sky was born. Within a year I had 1,000 members of staff signed up and a team of volunteers working alongside me (and our day jobs), to help grow the network. We went from strength to strength. Extending the initial online forum connecting parents from right across the organization (including contact centres, engineers, studios, retail and Head Office) to offer the following: webinars on topics like work-life balance; coffee mornings to bring people together in smaller groups; events with external speakers on topics like how children's brains develop; case studies to highlight different ways our parents were making it work; and even working with the facilities team to offer pregnancy parking (and if you're struggling with that one, try putting a basketball up your jumper when you next get out of your car in a tight space and you'll start to understand – wider spacers are a practical necessity in the later stages). However, most relevant was that we also partnered with an external supplier to offer workshops for those pre-, during and post-parental leave.

The impact these workshops had was really powerful, and repeatedly gave me my biggest sense of pride in what we had achieved because I could literally see the difference it was making to people. How much they took from the sessions. How it helped them to know they were not alone. How it empowered them to take control and gave them the confidence and motivation to take action.

As an independent Diversity and Inclusion Advisor, I now offer similar sessions to clients, both big and small. In either workshop or one-to-one format, these sessions offer support and guidance to new parents/parents-to-be, and their managers, when they take parental leave. And whilst the number of organizations recognizing the value in this kind of support is growing all the time, there are still a great many people working for organizations who do not (yet anyway).

Which brings me back to the idea of this book. Very simply, it is to package up the content of these sessions into a book format, so that access is no longer for those lucky few.

It is my sincere hope that you find it helpful. Whether you're taking leave yourself, your partner is or someone in your team is. My primary goal is to help people like you feel more confident and equipped to face the challenges of becoming a working parent. And to know not only can those challenges be overcome, but also that you will find you have grown as a person and therefore in your value as an employee.

The best result of all would be it leaving you feeling not just more confident but inspired to pay it forward. To connect with other working parents, share your own tips and learnings, help your organization do more. Lifting from a favourite quote by the inspirational speaker and author, Steve Maraboli, little acts can have a big impact...

> *Never decide to do nothing just because you can only do little.*
> *Do what you can. You would be surprised at what 'little acts'*
> *have done for our world.*

Introduction

You don't have to see the whole staircase,
just to take the first step.

(Martin Luther King)

Becoming a parent is a big step. Doing it while you're working makes that step feel all the bigger. And more of us than ever are choosing to take it. Opting to continue to work after having a child. Leaving and returning to our places of work. Choosing to embark on a life with dual roles: parent and employee.

Maternal employment rates have been on the rise for decades. In the UK, more than 75% of mothers now work, up from 66% in 2002.[1] And the figures are similar across the developed world.[2] The number of fathers working is also up, albeit by a smaller proportion.[3]

Governments and employers alike are supporting this trend with ever-improving national laws and practice around the world. There may (still) be huge variations in the amount of maternity/paternity/adoption leave, who can access it, how much is paid (and by who) and so on, but it's all moving in the right direction – to better support those working parents-to-be and improve employment rates, those of women in particular.

And whilst this is encouraging, taking time out from work when you start or add to your family is nevertheless a big deal for most people. Your concerns about leaving and returning to work may fade into the background of the main event at times, but they can come sharply back into focus at key points. And become really important to your overall experience. Everyone remembers how their boss reacted when they told them they were expecting to welcome a child to their family. Everyone remembers how well, or how badly, their organization handled their leave and return. And they talk about it. A lot. Because it ultimately has a big impact on us.

So, with that in mind, it is somewhat surprising we don't pay more attention to getting this element right. To making it a great experience for all. Or at least as good as it could be. Both from an individual point of view, and from an employer's viewpoint.

It might be because it can feel daunting. Where do you start? It can feel easier to muddle through. Or put your head in the sand: an all-too-common approach of managers, terrified of doing or saying the wrong thing. But like most complex challenges, it's usually easiest to break into small steps. Hence the quote.

How the book is structured

A series of small steps is exactly how I hope you'll view the structure of this book. Steps that make it easy to read. To pick and put down when you have a minute. And to refer back to when you need it.

The book is divided into three parts, to help you to navigate each of the key phases in turn: Before you go on leave; While you're away; and Returning to work.

Within each of these, there are a lot of subheadings and diagrams to break up the text. You'll also find checklist summaries that are like a workbook and exercises and tools to help you apply what you're reading to your own situation.

This is a really important point. Everyone's situation is unique. Your family set up. Your relationship with work. I have intentionally shared a lot of my own experiences, and those of others, because I wanted to make it easy to relate to and so, at times, it is very personal to me. But I also wanted to raise awareness of some of the differences; so where I've not had a personal experience, I have turned to others. Whether from sessions I have run or those who have very kindly let me grill them! The situations and sentiments are all very real, but I have left out names and details to protect confidentiality.

What this means, though, is not all these stories, or in fact the tips shared, will feel relevant to you. The references to breastfeeding, for example, are not going to be particularly helpful to you if you're a father in a same-sex relationship, or, like me, found you were unable to breastfeed. The same is true if I'm talking about a partner, and you don't have one. Feel free to skip over; I expect there will be other sections you'll read twice. Or better still, use them as an opportunity to learn about the challenges faced by others and/or think about how you might adapt a learning to your own circumstances.

Keeping in Touch (KIT) days are a great example of this. Never heard of them? You're probably not in the UK or Australia… but you might still find the concept appealing. And worth discussing with your employer, wherever you are in the world.

That doesn't mean this book can be viewed as a global reference source for entitlements for parental leave – the legal frameworks are too extensive and constantly changing (the good news being, mostly for the better). And for clarity, I am not a lawyer and therefore cannot offer legal advice. What I have done, though, is led with UK provisions and referenced others (that were correct at the time of writing) where I think they are helpful and thought-provoking. Where they might encourage debate about how they could be applied to your situation, your place of work or even your country. And I have provided links at the back for anyone looking for insight on the latest legislation in some of the key markets. The same is true for some of the language. You'll see I talk about 'breastfeeding' vs 'nursing' or 'lactation', 'prenatal' vs 'antenatal', 'nursery' vs 'daycare', 'annual leave' vs 'paid time off'. These are just different commonly used terms with the same meaning.

You may notice I refer to 'parental leave' more often than maternity, paternity, adoption or the myriad of options for sharing leave between partners that are available around the world. That, too, is intentional. It's hugely important to me that this book is gender neutral, and you are able to take out what's relevant and helpful to you.

You'll also pick up that this book is primarily aimed at those taking an extended period of parental leave, but the lines are not black and white here either. What might constitute a long period of leave in some countries (such as the US, for example), would be considered a short period of leave in others (such as the UK or Sweden). And if you work for a multinational organization, it may be different again – many have global policies on parental leave, meaning you may find yourself with far better support than is the norm in your country/state. Which brings us back to applying it to your unique situation. Your family. Your workplace.

And if you're wondering why the term **KIT days** is in bold, this is one of many glossary terms you'll find at the back of the book. They appear in bold to make them easy to identify and look up without losing your place. At the end of each chapter are key takeaways. For individuals taking leave, for their partners and for managers. If you're a skim reader, be sure to check these out. There's also a section at the end of each part where you can make your own notes which I strongly encourage you to do as you read. And if you're someone who can't bear to write in a book (it's taken me a while to convert!) you can download a handbook from my website at www. workingparents-to-be.com/handbook, or use the QR code below.

Finally, you'll find me talking about 'parents' a lot throughout. Obvious, you might think. This is a book primarily aimed at helping you if you're becoming a working parent! What I'm getting at is when you see 'parents', know I mean anyone who has parental responsibility. So that means you, whether you are a mother or a father. A single parent or one with a partner. Genetically related to your child or not. The primary caregiver or the secondary.

I have also intentionally used 'expecting' vs pregnant more, for the most part to reinforce this is for anyone about to welcome a child to their family – whether that's naturally through your own pregnancy, or through surrogacy or adoption. Similarly, you'll see I talk about 'becoming a parent', but that doesn't mean I'm not thinking about those for whom it's not their first.

You do, of course, have one major thing in common – you are all working parents – or are about to be.

When to read each part

This might sound an odd thing to call out, but when I run sessions I recommend the best time to have the pre-leave session, when to have the during-leave session and so on, so I feel it will be useful to share this here, too. Reading the insights and advice from the 'While you're away on parental leave' section won't be as effective when you're expecting as when you're starting to think about returning to work. You see my point? You may find yourself reading it all, then jumping back to key bits at the right time. And, as mentioned earlier, I've structured it with that in mind. So, when is the ideal time to read each part?

Part 1 – Before you go on leave: read any time from when you find out you're expecting until you start your leave. However, to get the most out of this try and make sure you've read this at least a month or two before you start your leave. This will give you more time to put what you've learned into practice.

Part 2 – While you're away on parental leave: ideally, read this section two to four months before you're looking to return to the workplace. Generally speaking, most people are not in the right headspace to absorb this in the first few months of their babies' lives. Equally, leaving it to the week before you return may mean you miss the opportunity to use it to help you inform your decisions and approach. That said, a lot of this clearly depends on where you are and so when it is normal to agree your return plan and how long you are away on leave – in countries where 12 weeks of leave is the norm your timescales are going to have to be squeezed in line with this.

Part 3 – Returning to work: read post-leave; sometime in the first couple of months of your return is perfect. Some people find it really helpful to do this as soon as they're back (and I would definitely at least skim it at this stage), but others find it helpful to read it more fully once they've had a few weeks back at work and have a better understanding of the challenges they're facing.

Part 1

Before you go on leave

Chapter 1

Being aware of the challenges ahead

Expecting a child when you're working brings many challenges. In this chapter, we take a look at the common challenges faced by parents-to-be and identify what your biggest concerns are at this point. The aim is to help you to: (a) realize you are not alone; and (b) become clearer on what's front of mind to help you work out a plan and overcome these challenges.

Where do we start?

If you're anything like me, the main thing on my mind once I'd announced to the team that I was having a baby was exactly that. I was having a baby! That, and how much I had to get done beforehand. Both at work and at home. On the work front, my main priority was getting everything tied up as much as possible and a smooth handover for anything else. I didn't give a lot of thought to coming back to work. I knew I wanted to return, but beyond that my thinking only stretched as far as entertaining the idea of working a 4-day week, instead of a 5-day week.

It's an exciting, exhausting and daunting time – often all at once. This makes it hard for your mind to naturally have the bandwidth for anything else. So, let's start by taking a step back, and thinking through the challenges you're likely to face at each stage.

The challenges pre-leave

Before you go on parental leave, the primary challenges you face are likely to be:

- Handling the various stakeholders
- Ensuring a smooth handover of your role

You'll also have to juggle prenatal/adoption appointments, and file key paperwork. Your experiences of these will be impacted by both your approach and the approach taken by your employer.

Some organizations are really well set up for employees when they become parents. They have well-trained HR teams; established procedures that guide you through what you need to do when; enhanced benefits; clear policies to refer to so you understand where you stand on everything from pay and pensions to taking leave for medical appointments; workplace assessments to keep you safe and well while performing your role; and the best even offer parental coaching and have family networks that will enable you to connect with other parents-to-be in your organization.

Other employers have very little formally in place. In either scenario, though, the biggest difference is often made by managers. All the policies and procedures in the world are no substitute for an empathetic leader who wants to help you through what is a life-changing experience.

This might leave you feeling you're at the mercy of your employer/ manager, and while that is partly true, this is where your own approach comes in. You are in a position to make a big difference to your own experience, and this starts before you go on leave.

The challenges during leave

While you're away from the organization on parental leave the most common challenges you're likely to face are:

- Adapting to the change
- Maintaining contact with work
- Preparing for your return

Having a child (or children) is life-changing – I don't think anyone would argue with that – but the impact on your relationship with your job, and your own identity, is less often acknowledged. Becoming a parent, whilst in some ways feeling like the most natural thing in the world, can to many still be a bit of a shock. How you feel about it, and adapt to it, is a very personal experience. It's also one that changes over time. How you feel in those early days, where the days and nights blur, and you are often both physically and emotionally exhausted, is likely to be different from how you feel in the latter weeks of your parental leave, when your focus is shifting to the next phase, your return.

How much you maintain contact with work will also change and be deeply personal. Some people want to switch off completely from work while on parental leave; others want to maintain contact socially with key members of their teams; and some want to stay in more regular touch. I always encourage new parents to take a complete break from work, at least to start with, to help them adapt to their new role as parent (or parent of more than one, if it's not your first) and enjoy it – as much as that is possible! There is no right or wrong here – it is your choice – but what's really important is proactively thinking about what you want that relationship to be and setting your own boundaries, from the start.

The same is true for your return. How much effort you put into thinking about your return is likely to make a big difference to how smooth that transition is – for you and those around you. There are, of course, some things you have to do, such as getting childcare arrangements in place. Others, like how you'll re-integrate yourself into the organization and manage the challenges of childcare hiccups, are perhaps less immediately obvious and you can find yourself winging it more than might feel comfortable.

And as you start thinking about these things, you'll quickly realize how many of them are linked. Take childcare, for example. Not only are there a huge variety of options and combinations, but these are also linked to finalizing your working arrangements and the date you go back. More so if you intend to make any changes. In turn, there are timelines you need to meet to agree your return and many childcare options fill up months in advance. The point being, preparing for your return isn't as simple as it might first seem, and the earlier you start thinking about it, the better.

The challenges post-leave

When you return to the organization, some of the key challenges you're likely to face are:

- Re-integrating back into the organization
- Adapting to your 'new normal'

Just as leaving the organization to spend your days looking after your new child/children is a big change, so is returning to the organization and learning to leave your child/children in the care of others. It's a transition some find easier than others, and one that is rarely a smooth path for anyone. There are trials along the way — some expected, some unexpected.

Since you left your role to go on leave there are likely to have been many changes: people joining and leaving the team you are part of; the organization having different priorities; revised objectives your team is responsible for; unfamiliar clients/stakeholders you'll need to work with; and even new systems to get to grips with. It can feel simultaneously like both the same place you left and a very different one. Some people will treat you as if you never left. Others will see you as a new starter. Of course, in reality, neither is right.

At the same time, you'll be adapting to your additional responsibilities outside of work. Most people find their working hours influenced by their childcare arrangements. You may need to drop off before work and pick up afterwards, and so often find yourself racing from A to B and longing for the days you didn't have to clock watch quite so urgently. And sometimes, of course, you'll have to drop everything to pick up earlier than expected when your child is unwell, which may be more often than you think at the beginning. All of this makes it harder to get back into the rhythm and start feeling part of the team as quickly as you might hope.

But as with the challenges at earlier stages, there are ways to make it easier to deal with them, which is the main aim of this book — to help you feel ready to face these challenges.

Exercise 1.1: How are you feeling right now?

Before we get too far into this, I want you to take a moment to think about the challenges you feel you are facing today – right now – and note them down. There is absolutely no right or wrong answer here. This exercise is purely intended as a way to capture your thoughts at this time and give you something to refer back to.

It's very likely that what you think is a challenge now will evolve over time. In fact, I would expect your views to change even in the amount of time it takes to read this book, let alone as you learn more from other sources, including those around you. Some of the challenges you note you will quickly overcome and tick off the list; others will raise their heads that you have not even thought of.

For now, though, I want you to ask yourself the following questions and write down the first thoughts that come to mind. Be really honest with yourself. No one else is going to read this list unless you choose to share it with them (although you might want to recruit your partner or a friend to help you do this). And no concern is too small. If it's bothering you, write it down. And look at this as a living list that grows with you. Revisit it often as you progress through the book and, if you find it helpful, add to it as you go.

What are your biggest concerns right now about leaving work?

What do you think your biggest concerns will be when you're thinking about returning to work?

Once you've done this, take a moment to process what's on your mind. Are there any themes emerging? For example, it could be a lack of information making you feel uneasy, or a particular relationship of concern. Or it might be a bunch of different things and that's okay, too. Either way, it's worth re-reading this a couple of times and letting it sink in. You can probably see where I'm going with this… being aware of what's worrying you is the first step to figuring out how to deal with it.

You might also be wondering if your concerns are the same as those of others. This is where a book can't replicate an in-person session, particularly a group session. Instead of doing this exercise alone, I encourage people to share their concerns. And very quickly everyone realizes how many concerns they have in common. But in the absence of that, yes, I would put money on you not being alone in how you're feeling about this!

The top 10 most common concerns at this point

To help further, below is a summary of the top 10 most common concerns I have heard raised at this point – and for your own benefit, try not to read this until you have attempted Exercise 1.1. I'm sharing this not to add worries to your list but with the hope it will reassure you. That some of the concerns listed will resonate with you (even if they're not top of your list right now). And that they may help you to see the perspective of others in the same boat.

1. Concern over whether your job will be there for you when you want to come back

OK, this is a big one. And without wishing to repeat myself, I think it's important to reiterate I am absolutely not looking to add to your list of worries or suggest you should be concerned about this. But, equally, I felt it important not to ignore a potential elephant in the room. This is the one many people have but few share – the worry that the person covering your role will do a better job than you. That they will realize they don't really need you.

Legally, of course, you are very well protected in most developed countries. Add to that, the vast majority of employers will value you and want you to come back. That said, the thought may cross the mind of even the most secure of us. It definitely crossed my mind. And it doesn't matter what level you're at, either. I've heard members of leadership teams voice this fear, 'Maybe they won't need me… ?', as well as those in more junior roles, who might typically feel the nature of their role means they are more easily replaced.

I think it's natural. You're leaving (albeit temporarily) a role you've worked hard to get – in some cases, really hard. It may feel very much part of who you are. Part of your identity. And now your responsibilities are either being handed to someone else or, in some instances, shared across multiple people in your absence. So, yes, you might find yourself wondering if your cover will be better than you. If the organization will find a way to do without you/your role. And that's very common and very normal.

2. Apprehension about what will change while you're on leave

You might also be concerned about the everyday organization changes that you won't be there to influence. Clients coming and going. Seeing projects through, taking on new ones. How your team works, the systems it uses. The list goes on.

Then there's feeling 'out of the loop' and not up to speed on the latest developments. And changes in personnel. People joining and leaving. You may wonder if you'll come back to a new manager. That's a big one for a lot of people. If you take a full year, there is a not insignificant chance that this might happen. If you have a great relationship with your current manager this can be a particularly unnerving prospect. More so still if you have agreed an informal agreement with them about your return before you go.

On a bigger scale, many organizations, especially larger ones, go through regular restructures. You may be concerned there will be one in your absence. It may even be underway when you go on leave. It might mean a change of role for you. It might even mean a promotion! But if this does happen, your employer should get in touch to keep you informed.

3. Feeling your manager doesn't know how to handle it

This can be very unsettling. As we noted earlier, your relationship with your manager is arguably the most influential in terms of your overall experience of going on leave and returning when you become a parent. Getting the impression that they are feeling unsure about how to handle it, what to say, what to do, will inevitably make you uneasy and could add to any feelings of insecurity you are experiencing about your future.

From their perspective there could be multiple reasons for this. You may be the first member of their team to be going on parental leave. Getting the news might have been a complete surprise and they need time to take it in. Their first thought might well have been: 'No! How will we manage without them?' Company policies and/or benefits may recently have changed and they might feel they don't know what they should. Very few managers intentionally handle this badly and it may be only a short-term challenge. Don't forget, in almost all cases you will have had significantly longer to get used to the idea than they have. However, the simple fact is some simply are not naturally as good at this as others – and for any managers reading and thinking, 'I hope that's not me', I hope you will feel more confident by the end of the book that it is not, or not any more at least.

4. Feeling you don't understand your rights/your company's policies

It's not just managers who feel not up to speed on company policies. It can feel like there's a whole new world of information you're expected to know. And perhaps the hardest part is that you don't know what you don't know. Everything from what official paperwork you need to submit and by when, to how do you juggle **prenatal appointments** (can you go in work time?), to what you will get paid and for how long. Some of this will be the same for everyone (within your country at least), regardless of where you work, and some of it will be specific to the organization you work for.

5. Not being able to take as much time off work as you want

There are typically two reasons that people feel like this. One is financial – that they don't feel they can afford to take off as much time as they would like to. Obviously, this is a very personal choice, and I do understand for some it won't even feel like a choice. It's simply reality. Particularly depending on where you work and where you are in the world and what's normal in terms of paid leave. However, for others it is more a choice about the type of lifestyle you lead and may require a close look at personal finances and some honest conversations at home.

The second is pressure to return. The important thing to be clear about here is if this is real or perceived. What I mean by that is that it's worth considering what it is that has made you feel that way. Are you putting pressure on yourself? And is this perhaps linked to your level of confidence that your role will be there when you get back? Or has someone said something directly to you? This is unlikely given the legalities, but the protections and how they are applied vary significantly across different countries, creating different social pressures.

Friends in the US, for example, tell me that while there is a federal law designed to make losing your job because you are pregnant illegal, there are ways around this, which in turn creates pressure to return more quickly; hence it's commonplace to do exactly that. More than half of mothers take less than nine weeks' leave in the US.[1] In Germany, on the other hand, parents can (and do) take up to three years off on parental leave – 45% of mothers whose youngest child is under three are on parental leave.[2] And of course, no one looks at these in isolation – financial and social pressures will be combined and play a key role in family decisions.

6. Concern that you won't be able to do your job with a child/on a flexible basis

Clearly, this depends a lot on the nature of your role as well as your childcare options and the cultural norms where you live. For some, any kind of flexibility feels unrealistic. Perhaps you work shifts or have clients in different time zones. Fitting that around childcare may at first appear impossible. Or it might be simply you are used to working long hours. And you feel this is now expected of you. It's an easy conclusion to jump to for some people. I have heard many times, 'I just can't see how I'll be able to continue to do my role as I have been' or words to that effect. Dig even a little under the surface and it's often not so clear cut.

> *I just can't see how I'll be able to continue to*
> *do my role as I have been.*
>
> (Parent-to-be, reflecting on their working pattern)

7. How you'll juggle everything

I'm intentionally calling this out separately because, rather than feeling you won't be able to do your role, it's about how you'll manage both roles: your role as an employee AND your role as a parent. And, for some, alongside that your role as a partner/ co-parent. This is perhaps the most common concern of all. And the most long lasting. Those with older children will tell you that, probably with a wry smile. Feeling you are successfully managing 'the juggle' is the holy grail of working parents. And in some ways just as unattainable – if, that is, you think you should be perfect at everything. Ask yourself – were you perfect in your role just as an employee before? Thought not. Keep that in your mind. And know this is a very real challenge for pretty much all working parents.

8. Worry your absence will affect your career progression

Another big one. It's hard not to fear being 'out of sight, out of mind'. This can be particularly acute for those working in organizations with set annual promotion rounds or going through imminent restructures. It's also something that plays on the minds of those considering a more flexible working arrangement. Whether that's working fewer hours, working different hours or just in a different way than you have before – which to be brutally honest will be most people. You may fear working part time will mean 'opportunities will pass me by'. Or that leaving a meeting that's running over to get to nursery pick-up on time will be held against you.

There's also the fear that simply being out of the organization for an extended period will 'set you back' and mean you have to 'prove yourself' all over again.

9. Unease about getting childcare in place

When you're expecting a child, and planning to return to work, you are, of course, very conscious that you will need childcare. For many people, though, what that childcare looks like is pretty fuzzy at this point. It can also be a source of growing concern as you start to reframe your thinking around how your new world will work. But it's also easy to push to the back of your mind and focus on the imminent arrival. Which for many makes it one of those nagging fears. Others feel it more strongly, particularly if they don't have immediate family support locally, if one or both partners travel a lot for work, if finances are really tight or your period of leave relatively short and/or options locally are limited.

10. Anxiety over the plans (or lack of) for you to hand over your role

Naturally, the closer to the child's arrival you get, the more this becomes a priority. If you don't have a plan in place, or feel it's not set in stone, or hasn't been communicated, this can start to cause a lot of angst. No one wants to go off on leave feeling there are loose ends.

And it's not just the day-to-day workload. A big part of your handover is telling key people that you're going. I've been surprised by how many people I've spoken to who have felt it's unclear who's responsibility it is to tell extended teams/clients etc. or don't know who they're handing over to until the last minute. And this is both individuals going on leave and managers. It sometimes seems to fall between the cracks, and more remote working hasn't helped. If you don't see someone in person for a while, they may not see you are pregnant/have the small talk opportunity to learn you are becoming a parent. And then one day you are gone and it's a shock and they wonder what's happened to you!

Key takeaways from this chapter

- It's worth spending some time at the beginning thinking through the challenges you will face before, during and after your leave
- Identifying those most relevant to you will help you build a plan to overcome them
- Remember, you will not be the only one feeling this way
- The good news is that you will quickly be able to overcome some concerns. Others will prove to be longer-term challenges, but there are ways to overcome them.

If you're supporting your partner/someone close to you

Try and make them feel less alone, right from the start. Help them identify and face what the biggest challenges will be for them and how these might change over time. Keep checking in and start thinking – how you could support them in overcoming these challenges? And don't forget about you in this – what concerns do you have at this point?

If you're supporting someone in your team

Think about which of the concerns raised might be front of mind for them and start thinking about what you could do to address them. What would it take? What could you do to take one off their list of concerns?

Chapter 2

Developing your support network

We know there are challenges ahead. The next obvious questions are, how does that translate into the sort of support you will need and who is in a position to help you? The good news is there are many sources of support you can draw on at this time. In this chapter, we'll take a look at the type of support you might need, how to identify who could help and how to make sure they are as receptive as possible when you need them.

What type of help might you need?

There are many ways people can help you:

- **Practically** – such as helping you get an understanding of your company's policies and benefits and what you need to do and when; helping you with financial planning and how you'll manage while you're on leave (particularly if you will get little or no pay in that time); sharing advice, for example on childcare options; looking after your child/children when you can't or need a break; and even just picking up nappies or medication when you're in the thick of it.

- **Emotionally** – by, for example, coming with you to prenatal/hospital appointments and classes; sharing their experiences and advice; being a shoulder to cry on or just listening when you're having a tough day.
- **Professionally** – perhaps helping you work through a problem such as how to manage a difficult stakeholder whose meeting you can no longer make because you have to go pick up a sick little one; acting as a mentor to discuss your career aspirations; or helping you look at your workload objectively and make some judgement calls on priorities.

This list isn't exhaustive, but hopefully you get the idea. And if your mind is already coming up with a list of the type of help you think you might need, note it down.

Who might be able to help you?

Let's start with those around you at work. Perhaps the most important in many ways is your manager, but they are far from the only one; there'll be people in your HR team who are responsible for handling your leave and who are likely to be one of the best sources of information about what happens to your pay and benefits; then there are members of senior management/your directors; there will be members of your team, both peers and direct reports (if you have them); and then there are clients and suppliers. All these people can be a source of either support or influence – or both.

But it doesn't stop here. There will be lots of people outside of work who can help you too; your partner (if you have one); parents; friends (with and without children of their own); your doctor; those you've met through prenatal classes/other organizations and so on.

Exercise 2.1: Who might be able to help you?

Let's start by creating a list of stakeholders both inside and out of work who are in a position to help you through this transition. Remember, you will need different types of support at different times, so don't discount any at this point. You're essentially creating a list that you can look back at when you need it (even metaphorically). Use the suggestions in the box below to help you.

Sources of Support – pointers to get you started

Work	Home
Manager	Partner
Director/leadership	Parents
Work friends/colleagues	Close friends
HR partner/manager/contact	Brother(s)/sister(s)/cousin(s)
Key clients/suppliers	Prenatal class members

How do you identify the key ones?

In a moment, I'm going to introduce you to another exercise to identify which of these relationships it would help to give more attention to. But before we do that, I wanted to take the opportunity to focus in on that one really key relationship in all of this – the one you have with your manager.

Why? Because, for most people, whether they have a good or bad experience of parental leave is in large part determined by their relationship with their manager. In fact, if I ask people, I usually get one of two responses: 'it was great, my manager was so supportive' or 'not the best to be honest, my manager's heart was in the right place, but they didn't seem confident to engage' (or words to that effect – sometimes worse in truth).

This is what makes it such an important relationship to put effort into before you go on leave, especially if it's not the strongest to begin with. To help that, I want to take a moment to explore the perspective of a manager, when you take parental leave.

> *My manager's heart was in the right place, but they didn't seem confident to engage.*

(Mum on leave, reflecting on the level of support from their manager)

The perspective of your manager

As the quote above suggests, the majority of managers do not intentionally handle this badly. Of course not. They want to do the right thing. Often, they are afraid. Afraid of saying or doing the wrong thing. Of not knowing what the policies are and so how to answer your questions. Afraid of losing you. Wondering how they will fill the gap while you're away.

They will also often find themselves in tricky situations. Perhaps you've told a friend at work before you've officially shared your news and they've not been completely discreet, so your manager knows, just not officially. Or they desperately want to ask how long you'll be off so they can put the right cover in place, but they are aware they can't put pressure on you so don't know how to phrase this.

Try and bear all of this in mind, and from the outset establish an open and honest dialogue with your manager – it really will make a big difference for you, and for them.

And if you're really unlucky, and do have a bad apple, they will still have motivations you can consider objectively to minimize the impact. And there are others you can turn to.

Your other supporters

So, who are the other key ones? Have a look at your list of people from Exercise 2.1 and think about who could potentially be in the best position to help. Start by considering whether they are:

1. Currently a big supporter or not, and if not, why not
2. How much impact they have/how much of a difference they could make to your experience

The aim here is to help you work out which are going to be the key relationships and what you can do to get the best out of them.

Exercise 2.2, Part 1: How much support could they offer and how much influence do they have?

Start by reviewing your draft list of stakeholders both inside and out of work who are in a position to help you through this transition (using your list from Exercise 2.1).

Now think about how supportive you think they currently are and how much potential to make a difference to you they have. What I'm getting at here is that there will be some obvious points of support you will naturally turn to, but these are not the only ones. There may be others who are less obvious – either in terms of you thinking of asking them for help or them being inclined to give it – but who could make a big difference to you. Thinking through who they might be now could be of great help to you later.

Now, plot those names onto this framework:

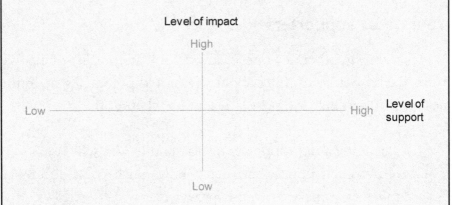

Level of impact

High

Low ——————————————————————— High   Level of support

Low

Level of impact – refers to how much of a difference they could make to your experience

Level of support – refers to how supportive you feel they are of you becoming a parent

For example, your manager may not (from your perspective) appear to be very understanding or supportive and yet they may have a big influence on your overall experience as well as your future career progression; so in this example, you'd put them in the top left segment. Or, you may have a director/ senior manager, who has always been a bit of a mentor and is a parent to a young child themselves. They may not be able to directly influence your day to day, but they could be a real champion able to influence your manager, so they'd go to the right and above the line. Or there may be a colleague who has been there and done that with going on parental leave and could share lots of useful tips, so you'd put them bottom right. I've added these to the example framework that follows so you can see how this builds.

This clearly isn't an exact science. Even as I wrote this, I challenged myself on where to 'put' people. For example, the friend who has been there and done that could be hugely impactful if they are able to help when you face a major challenge, but hopefully you get the point. Take a look at the example framework and the pointers to get you started.

Example template

Level of impact

Now you have plotted them, if you're comfortable I'd recommend doing part 2 of the exercise with someone close to you. It could be a colleague or your partner. You may want to use your judgement based on the most contentious choices.

Exercise 2.2, Part 2: What would it take to get the most support from them?

Review your stakeholder map/framework and think/talk through the following for each name:

- Why have you put them in that quarter?
- How are they likely to be feeling about you becoming a parent and why?

- What could you do to get the best out of the relationship at this time?
- What would it take to move them into or keep them in the Champion/Supporter quarter?

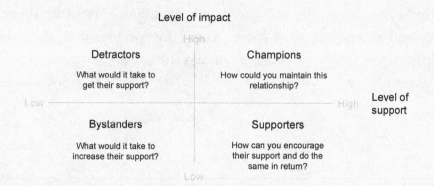

Level of impact

High

Detractors

What would it take to get their support?

Champions

How could you maintain this relationship?

Low ———————————————————— High

Level of support

Bystanders

What would it take to increase their support?

Supporters

How can you encourage their support and do the same in return?

Low

For example, it may be your manager is just feeling concerned about how they will cope without you and worried about saying the wrong thing. Be careful not to make any assumptions. Talk to them and try and find out. Being open about how you're feeling and what you're comfortable talking about with them might really help break down any barriers. Equally, to keep your director in the top right, it might be helpful to keep them updated on your progress, and share your thoughts on career progression or even get their advice on making sure you're not forgotten while you're away. And that colleague who has been there and done that? Make an effort to get to know them better, ask their advice. Every parent LOVES to share their best tips! Who knows, they could become a great friend who gets what you're going through in a way others without children may not.

And if you're feeling this seems a bit calculating, it's not meant to be. The majority of those around you really will want to help you. This is just a way to remind yourself who is in your life that can help you, and to think about it from their perspective so that they are able to give you that help.

My final point on this subject, which is a big one, is please do ask for and accept help. For some people, myself included, it can be difficult to accept help, let alone ask for it. So, to repeat, most people genuinely want to help you – so let them. Everybody wins.

Key takeaways from this chapter

- Think carefully about the type of help you most need
- Consider who might be in a position to help you and what their perspective might be – especially your manager
- Don't make assumptions
- Think about what it would take to keep or even increase the support of key people
- Ask for and accept help

If you're supporting your partner/someone close to you

Help them think this through and encourage them to include everyone who might be in a position to help. Be honest with yourself – where do you think you sit on the scale of support and influence? What would it take to motivate you to be more supportive still? What support might you need yourself? Who would be in a position to help you and what are their motivations likely to be?

If you're supporting someone in your team

Ask yourself if you're doing all you can to support them. And be aware of all the other potential sources of support in your workplace. It might be they extend beyond your immediate team. What can you do to help them directly and how could you encourage them to seek support elsewhere? Are there people you could connect them with who could be helpful? Do you have insights into the motivations of those who are in a position to influence their careers that you could share with them?

Chapter 3

Building a plan, working out what to do when

Now we have an idea of the challenges ahead and who you might look to for help, how do you approach this? What do you do first? In this chapter, we'll go through a step-by-step checklist to help you break it down into manageable chunks. Some of these you may already be on top of. Others you may not have thought of yet. Some will require more work than others. Or feel more important to you. This is *not* meant to be a to-do list (although you can use it that way if that works for you, hence the checkboxes). Look at it instead as a guide. A way to gauge how you're feeling about each area and what you feel it would be helpful for you to tackle. And do use the handbook or section at the end of Part 1 to make your own notes.

Making sure you're informed

As we saw earlier, some of the common concerns raised relate to feeling somewhat daunted by all the policies and procedures. There's a lot of terminology to get your head around. Timelines you need to be aware of. And, of course, these are not just the policies of the country you live in as the organization you work for will also have policies, benefits and ways of doing things specific to them. It can feel overwhelming, particularly if you're pregnant and feeling really tired or experiencing physically debilitating symptoms such as nausea. More generally, it's also not information all neatly packaged up for you. This, of course, depends a lot on the individual organization and the manager, but when you don't know what you don't know, it can be tricky to work through this. Sky, as you might expect, was pretty organized. That said, I still found myself confused over what happened to my pay when I went on leave and unaware of the conditions around adding my newborn to my health insurance, for example. Even with the best intentions and most prepared organizations, things can fall through the net.

So, where do you start?

☐ Work out what parental leave is available to you

How much leave is available to you, and which is applicable to you will depend on where you live, your own situation (whether you're pregnant, going through fertility treatment, adopting, using a surrogate…) and the organization you work for.

As the 'Explainer' box below outlines, there is a considerable difference in provision in different countries and this is constantly changing – happily, mostly for the better, but that makes it impossible to list here. You will find links at the back of the book to use as a starting point if you're not sure where to look, which I hope are helpful. If you work for a larger organization, the HR team there should also be a great place to get information. They can obviously also advise on any enhanced benefits your employer offers.

Explainer: Global variations in support for new parents

Support for new parents varies hugely across the world. Not just **maternity leave**, and whether it exists in the first place or is paid (in part or full), but that of **paternity leave**, the availability of equal levels of support when adopting, or for same-sex couples. Time off for prenatal appointments, protection in your job – or against losing it – when pregnant. Time off for breastfeeding. The availability of **emergency leave** and whether it's automatically paid or not. And **parental leave** – in its narrower definition, i.e. time off, paid or unpaid, for parents. In some countries, such as Germany and Sweden, it is normal to use this as part of the overall period of leave, whereas in others, like the UK, it is used a separate leave entitlement to support parenthood in the older years.

What these policies are and how they are used varies widely, but the good news is they are getting better all the time. To give you some context, the International Labour Organization (ILO, which is a UN agency) has conducted surveys of 185 countries, in 2011 and 2021. They report that as of 2021 the global average duration of maternity leave was 18 weeks, and for paternity leave it was 9 days (1.3 weeks). However, both have risen in that decade, as have how much is paid and how many countries offer it.[3]

Some countries are lauded for their progressive policies and others, notably the US, are berated. The lack of national paid parental leave in the US is well known. What is perhaps less well known is that an increasing number of US states are bringing in their own paid family leave laws. Finding out what is available to you – when you need it – is therefore really important, particularly as it may have recently changed.

☐ Make sure you know what you have to do when

Speak to your manager or HR team to find out what forms you'll need to complete, what the deadlines are and how they want you to submit them.

If you're pregnant, one of the most important in the UK for example, is the **MAT B1**, or Maternity Certificate. Your doctor will give this to you if you're pregnant at around 20 weeks and you need to submit this in order to qualify for **Statutory Maternity Pay** (SMP) or **Maternity Allowance** (MA). It's basically an official confirmation that you are pregnant and when your due date is. Your employer needs this to officially record you as going on maternity leave and for their records with HM Revenue & Customs (HMRC) so that you are paid any Statutory Maternity Pay you are due, if appropriate. It will also open up your eligibility for other maternity benefits and rights (such as any enhanced pay and benefits your organization offers).

You will also need to let them know when you want to start your maternity leave and do this by at least 15 weeks before your due date. Usually, the earliest you can start your leave is 11 weeks before your baby is due.

The same is true for paternity leave. If your partner is pregnant, you must apply for paternity leave and **Paternity Pay** at least 15 weeks before your baby is due.

There are special provisions if your baby is very early or you experience other complications or, in the worst-case scenario, pregnancy loss.

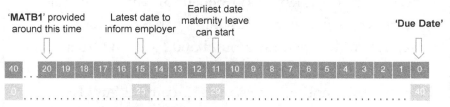

If you're using a surrogate

The process is relatively similar if you're using a surrogate, although you shouldn't be asked to provide a MAT B1 (a surrogate has the same rights to leave as those having their own children, so she'll need this for her employer). You may, however, find your employer doesn't have a specific 'Surrogacy Leave' policy yet – many organizations are rapidly announcing these or more inclusive 'Family Leave' policies – but either way, you do still need to notify your employer and choose which partner takes **Statutory Adoption Leave** (SAL) and which one of you takes **Paternity Leave** – i.e. who's going to be the primary carer. The former could entitle you to **Statutory Adoption Pay** (SAP), the latter **Statutory Paternity Pay** (SPP) and you can choose to take **Shared Parental Leave** (SPL) as well. Once the baby is born you will also need to apply to make you the child's legal parent(s) by either applying for a **Parental Order** if one of you is genetically related to the child or go through the adoption process if neither of you are.

Explainer: Surrogacy

As defined by Wikipedia, 'Surrogacy is an arrangement, often supported by a legal agreement, whereby a woman agrees to delivery/labour on behalf of another couple or person, who will become the child's parent(s) after birth'. It is still relatively rare (only around 500 Parental Orders were registered in the UK in 2020) but a rapidly growing way to have a baby – not just for same-sex couples but also those in mixed-sex relationships along with single parents-to-be.[4]

Often, but not always, at least one parent is genetically related to the child. As such, unlike adoption, the intended parent(s) are able to be at the birth and effectively become the baby's parent(s) from day one.

If you're adopting

Adoption is similar in terms of deciding which partner is the 'main adopter' and therefore entitled to **adoption leave**, but it's trickier when it comes to timelines as they are less clear. Whilst the early steps are typically well documented (application process, training sessions, home visits etc.), once you're approved, you could be matched at any time. One father I spoke to explained how difficult this can be when considering when to start adoption leave, particularly if you're in a more senior role:

The first question my boss asked was 'when are you going to be out?' and I couldn't answer that.

(Adoptive dad)

There could be months or even years between being approved and finding out you have been matched and therefore wanting to start your leave. Working out a plan with your manager that works for you both will be even more important in this scenario.

☐ Get an understanding of what happens to your pay and other benefits while you're on leave

If you're pregnant in the UK, as long as you were in employment for at least 26 weeks when you are in the 15th week before your baby is due, you will be entitled to Statutory Maternity Pay (SMP). To be eligible for Statutory Adoption Pay, you need to have been continuously employed by your employer for at least 26 weeks by the week you were matched with a child. Eligibility for Statutory Paternity Pay falls in line with whether your partner is taking maternity or you're adopting. Other countries have different provisions and eligibility requirements, but you can see with just one example, it can take a minute to get your head around.

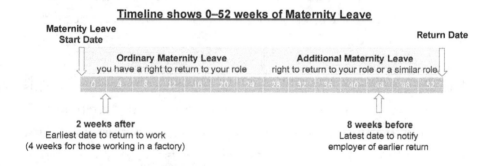

Depending on the organization you work for and how long you've been there you may also be entitled to enhanced pay. Some organizations pay this weekly to keep it simple when calculating pay alongside statutory pay.

This can be confusing if you're used to being paid monthly – which is exactly what happened to me. I went happily off on maternity, was fully focused on my imminent arrival, and then was a little thrown when my pay didn't arrive the date that I was expecting it and when it did arrive it was for a different amount. It took a few phone calls to understand what had happened. Fortunately, my daughter arrived later than her due date, so I had some time to get to the bottom of it, but I highly recommend pre-empting that one!

Similarly, it's worth understanding what will happen to any discretionary bonuses and other benefits such as a company pension, company car or private health insurance that may be impacted by going on leave. I discovered, for example, that my private health cover would cover my daughter, but that I had to add her within three months of her birth. I could very easily have missed that.

The simplest way to do this is to meet with either your manager or someone in your HR team, go through all your benefits one by one according to your situation and establish what happens to them. Don't be afraid to ask. It makes life simpler for everyone if you know what to expect.

And spare a thought for how your tax bill will be affected too. This will depend a lot on how much pay you receive, and when, but it's worth looking into. If, for example, you are on parental leave for a year and this falls across two tax years (as is likely), you may find you have overpaid tax in the first year – the government cannot predict how long you'll be off so they tax you as normal and only correct it afterwards. Worth exploring.

☐ Familiarize yourself with the relevant policies

It's helpful to find out early on what your organization's policy is on things like prenatal appointments. All organizations are required by law to give you time off for these appointments, and as far as I can work out this seems to apply globally to most developed countries in some form or another (in the US it's covered by the Family and Medical Leave Act [FMLA]). In the UK, this is paid time off for pregnant employees, but partners are generally only allowed to attend two appointments (typically choosing the scans) and it's at the employer's discretion (and often the manager's) whether that leave is paid or not. And, of course, this assumes there are no added complications.

Adoption is a little harder. The adoption process is a big commitment in itself and whilst in the UK, if you are the main adopter, you have the right to paid time off for five adoption appointments after you've been matched with a child, there is no such provision before.

In the world of hybrid working, or if your organization operates a policy of unlimited leave, on the face of it this can seem even more complicated. However, all of this just reinforces how important it is to establish clear and open communications with your manager and HR team right from the start so that if you need it, you know exactly who to talk to and you can agree how you approach it with minimal stress on either side.

Speaking of complications, I feel I should also advise you to read this early on so that you know what support is available should the worst happen. The last thing you'll want to be doing is trying to understand how much paid leave you'll have etc. In that scenario, you'd obviously hope your manager/HR team will be on top of this, compassionate and prepared. However, it's not a given, so spending a few moments just checking where you would stand could be time very well spent – even if none of us ever wants to think about this. It's also worth flagging that if you're advised that for medical reasons you need to start your parental leave suddenly, this can be very challenging. One mother explained: 'I had one day to try and hand over everything, and even that I had to negotiate with the doctor.' There is obviously a limited amount you can do in this scenario – you have to put your health first – but it reinforces the point, the earlier you can do your homework, the better.

> *I had one day to try and handover everything, and even*
> *that I had to negotiate with the doctor.*
>
> (Mum-to-be of twins, experiencing complications)

On a more positive note, some organizations offer amazing benefits specific to pregnant employees like pregnancy yoga or pregnancy parking – yes, if you're pregnant and drive to work you will need more space to get out of your car! I found it really hard to get my head around the fact I was suddenly wider front to back than side to side, meaning squeezing through narrow spaces required a different approach…

There may also be services you might find yourself really valuing that you haven't before, like on-site massage services. And, of course, again depending on your work environment, you may benefit from a risk assessment (or at least a conversation with your manager if you work in a small business without these kind of formal processes). I have clients in the construction industry where the need is perhaps more obvious, but even in an office environment you may find you need a different chair or footstool to help make you more comfortable. It's worth reviewing what's available so you're aware of them as your needs change.

Finally, looking further ahead, if you're planning on breastfeeding on your return, it's worth finding out what provisions there are for you, both in terms of facilities for pumping and storage and also time. In many countries, there is a right to paid nursing breaks. In Spain, for example, working mothers are entitled to 2x30 minute breaks per day or to finish 30 minutes early for feeding. There is a similar provision in China.[5] In the UK, whilst there is no specific provision, there are other legal protections, and more and more organizations are making sure they can accommodate these needs.[6] It is worth checking out and speaking to other parents before you go on leave to find out how these work in practice in your organization.

☐ Agree with your manager when and how you share your news

When you break the news of your pregnancy/that you're becoming a parent with your manager, it's a good idea to talk to them about how you share the news with your team and beyond. This is particularly important if you feel strongly about sharing this news personally with key people, and/or if you taking parental leave is going to raise concerns about who will cover your role in your absence. Agreeing a plan together so that you are aligned on who will know – and when – will help you feel in control and able to fully enjoy what is wonderful news to share.

And if you're wondering about the legalities... there are set timelines for you to tell your employer. In the UK, you must tell your employer about the pregnancy at least 15 weeks before the beginning of the week the baby is due. Bear in mind that in practice this means by 25 weeks, when you're likely to have a very obvious bump, so they will probably have guessed by then, anyway! There is no rule saying when you should tell your employer before that.

A lot of women wait until after the 12-week scan, but if you're struggling with symptoms and need additional support it may be worth telling them before this time. In terms of telling others, legally this is considered personal information, so your manager and HR team *should* keep it confidential. I say *should*, as they may not be aware of this, so addressing the issue when you share your news avoids any miscommunication.

To link back to a point from earlier, do think carefully before sharing your news with others at work before you manager. It could put them in a difficult position if they find out and know, but not officially.

If you're adopting or using a surrogate

Adoption and surrogacy bring their own challenges to this moment. You may want to be really open with your employer, or at least your boss, particularly given the training days adoption often requires. But then again, you might also be worried about how this news could be met, given the timeframes involved. One father using a surrogate told me: 'I decided to keep the whole part of this journey to myself until we had a positive pregnancy test' and expressed guilt at feeling they were 'keeping something from my boss' but 'didn't want to be held back at work, passed over for opportunities'. It's an understandable dilemma. On the one hand, most people want to be open, share what they're going through and gain support from those around them, but the near certainty of timescales (and outcome) following a pregnancy scan is very different to that of IVF or adoption.

> *I decided to keep the whole part of this journey to myself until we had a positive pregnancy test.*
>
> (Dad of two, who used a surrogate)

If you're a single parent

Sharing the news that you're expecting when you're single can bring some interesting reactions. My favourite, that one **solo parent** was kind enough to share, was 'Oh, I didn't know you got married!'. Cue awkward moment. It's another point where it's very easy to make assumptions. And get caught out by that.

If you're expecting it to be a surprise and you want to avoid an uncomfortable moment, it's worth considering a simple one-liner to address it as you deliver the news, something along the lines of: 'I've got some news, I've been wanting to be a parent for a while now and have decided to go for it alone – and I'm pregnant/ adopting!'

Oh, I didn't know you got married!

(Solo parent-to-be)

If you're going through IVF

I can relate to this personally as we went through IVF, not with my daughter, but when we were trying for a second and struggling to get (and stay) pregnant. As anyone who has experienced IVF will tell you, it's both physically and emotionally tough and not something everyone wants to tell the world about. And it can be an extended process over months or even years. I was fortunate that I had a reasonable amount of flexibility to make the necessary appointments and found it easier to keep work separate, aside from sharing this with a few trusted colleagues.

The decision to tell a few people was partly based on an earlier experience of pregnancy loss. Having experienced challenges getting pregnant a second time, we were so elated, and it somehow felt so much more precious, that we chose not to tell anyone until after the scan. We didn't get as far as the scan. Losing the baby was one of the hardest things I've ever been through. Having to tell people who didn't know I was even pregnant made it that much harder.

The main point is there is no right or wrong here – focus on what's best for you and your family. What will provide you with the support you need, both personally and professionally.

☐ If you feel you're at risk of discrimination

This is a tough one and, as I said, I'm not a lawyer; however, I am very aware that, sadly, many new parents or parents-to-be have negative experiences, some of which are discriminatory. According to the Equality and Human Rights Commission, it affects some 390,000 pregnant women and new mothers in the UK each year, so it's not a small problem.[7] It's therefore a potential elephant in the room I wanted to address.

I wouldn't be writing this book if I didn't believe the approaches I've recommended couldn't make a difference to a great many people, and their experiences of parental leave, but I also recognize that some may find themselves in very tough situations for which this does not help. If that is you, I would encourage you to seek specialist help. Find out your rights to help you make informed decisions about what you can (and can't) do about it – and off the back of that, what's best for you and your family. That help is out there, and there's more than ever before. You'll find some links at the back that I hope are a good starting point.

Doing some preparation – at work

Whilst sharing your news with your employer has probably felt like a huge milestone, and perhaps one you are very relieved to have out of the way, what you can do to help make the transition over the next few months smoother for you and the organization doesn't stop there. Not everything I will cover in this section is something you have to do. But it's well worth reviewing each of them and deciding if they're something that you feel could make a difference for you.

☐ Consider if you'd like to be involved in arranging cover while you're on leave

Most roles will require someone else to cover them in your absence. Strictly speaking, this is your manager's responsibility. However, it may be in your interests to help them with this and work on it together. For example, you can use it as an opportunity to review how you spend your time and what the priorities will be going forward. Let's face it, very few of us end up doing exactly what it says in our job description on a day-to-day basis! Sometimes that's deliberate and welcome. Often, it's just how the role has evolved and you, as an individual, have grown and developed. It's great to take stock of that and agree with your manager what form that cover should take and even the focus of the role for the future.

You may also want to be involved in the hiring process. Interviewing potential candidates. You know your job better than anyone else so can be a great help to your manager with this. And having a good relationship with that person from the start can make your handover at the beginning and end of your leave that much easier.

☐ Create a handover plan and agree this with your manager

Getting agreement on a handover plan is really important for both you and your manager, and beyond that, your wider team and stakeholders. It can be easy to slip into focusing on meeting particular deadlines or delivering specific projects without thinking much beyond that. Before you know it, your last day is here, and other elements may have been forgotten.

Fully review your role and what needs to be handed over to whom, and almost as importantly, when. I always recommend having this in place at least six weeks before your last day, but it's never too soon to have a plan in place. Once you've told everyone, it can often feel like everything goes back to normal for quite a long time. So much so that when your last week arrives it feels like a shock. Creating a handover plan together can be a really helpful way to focus everyone's mind on the fact that you are actually going and what's left to do before.

Consider who else would benefit from seeing this too. Sharing certain elements is likely to really help you manage the expectations of key stakeholders – whether they are external clients, key suppliers or wider team members. They will all be wondering what happens while you're away. Showing everyone you have a plan will both reassure and may even highlight anything you and your manager have overlooked and flush out concerns you can address.

☐ Agree a final date and consider ramping down in your final weeks

I say a final date as I mean the last date you will work before you begin your parental leave but, officially, in the UK at least, it's the

start date you need to agree. If you're pregnant, legally you are supposed to agree the date you plan to start maternity leave no later than 15 weeks before your baby is due; however, in practice you can obviously amend this, particularly if your baby arrives early. The same is true if you're using a surrogate. For Shared Parental Leave (SPL) it's eight weeks before you plan to start your leave. For adoption, it's 28 days, although again in practice you may find your employer exercises some discretion here.

The obvious question to ask yourself is how much time, if any, do you want on leave before your due date? And I appreciate the question here is financial as well as emotional. The less obvious question is do you want to work up to that date in the same capacity as now? And by that I mean if, for example, you currently work full time, do you want to work full time until your last day or would it be helpful to reduce your hours/days in those last few weeks? (And I realize as I write this that those in countries like the US who work for employers giving them no paid leave may read this section in some shock of what is available elsewhere and what I'm about to suggest!)

Many women find getting around increasingly difficult in the later stages of pregnancy and are very tired. If you're either keen to keep working as close as possible to your due date, or perhaps need to financially, reducing your hours can be a good compromise. This is clearly something you would need to agree with your employer, but many are open to discussing this, particularly if it means you starting your leave a little later and buying them more time with you in the team. And this is not just for pregnant women. If you're adopting or using a surrogate, you might still want to factor in some preparation time.

It can also be done using annual leave so your pay isn't impacted. And if you're worried about your annual leave allowance, remember to factor in that you may have the whole year's allowance to use. Very few people have their child in sync with their organization's annual leave calendar! For example, if you're in the UK, your organization's annual leave calendar runs January to December and you start your parental leave in July, you will have the full allowance available to you to use from January to June. That's a lot of leave... more on this later (see Chapter 6), as there are other creative ways to make the most of this and help you make the transition. For now, something to start thinking about.

☐ Consider the use of KIT days while you're on leave

Keeping in Touch days or KIT days are a UK provision designed to help you do exactly that. Keep in touch with your workplace while you're on parental leave, or more specifically maternity or adoption leave. You can choose to work up to 10 KIT days during your leave – either individual days or in blocks. If you're on SPL, it's 20 days and they are called **Shared Parental Leave in Touch days** (SPLIT days). These are in addition to the 10 KIT days – so, yes, that means in theory 30 days you can choose to work – and be paid – while you're on parental leave (although I have yet to meet someone who has used this many!). The really important word here though is 'choose' – both KIT days and SPLIT days are optional on both sides, i.e. they have to be agreed by both you and your employer. They cannot force you to work a KIT or SPLIT day any more than you can force them to allow you to.

That said, they're a great way to help you reconnect with your team and the organization, and in my experience, employers have embraced them and encourage their use. Exactly how you use them is again up to you and your manager to agree, but a few examples of ways to use them include coming along to a team offsite/strategy/planning meeting; going on a training course; having a handover with your cover. You can also use them as a way to 'ramp up' – more on this later (see Chapter 6).

If you think this is something you might be interested in, it's a great idea to have a conversation with your manager and see if they like the idea too. And then you can start exploring together how you might use them. Much easier to have a brief conversation now than leave it until you're on leave and have a little one to look after. It will also help keep you front of mind when you're on leave and in the few months before you return, so that you're invited to key events.

And if you're reading this outside the UK or Australia (the two countries I am aware of that currently offer this provision), don't necessarily just skim over this. I know of at least one new parent who asked about this in the US and their organization agreed it was a great idea and so they worked out a way to make it happen.

☐ Think about how you want to be contacted while you're on leave

If you don't discuss this with your manager before you go on leave, there is risk that assumptions will be made. And, personally, I believe assumptions are something you want to avoid, particularly when it comes to parental leave.

In my experience, managers tend to assume that they shouldn't contact you whilst you're on leave. And those on leave want some kind of contact. Even if it's just social to keep up with friends in the team. So, as you can see, there's already a disconnect.

Legally (in the UK), you and your employer have the right to reasonable contact while you're on leave. However, somewhat unhelpfully there are no definitions of what that is. Common sense tells you (and my belief is this is the intention behind it) the legislation is designed to help you have a total break from work, if that is what you want, and leave it open to individuals to agree what that looks like. So, this is very much up to you to decide in terms of what you're contacted about, when and how.

What you're contacted about

Let's start with the 'what'. If you do want contact, it might be just social contact – for example, hearing when a team member gets married or has a baby or being invited to the Christmas party or monthly team lunch/drinks. You may want to bring your child to your workplace – or you may not. You might also want to be kept in the loop on team changes. Of course, if this directly affects you/your role, your manager should be keeping you informed, but there might be changes affecting the wider team that they consider less directly relevant, but all the same, you might want to know about – such as team promotions, new clients or even a company takeover etc. At the other extreme, some people want to stay on top of everything. For anyone feeling pressure at this point, in my experience very few fall into this category and they are typically those taking minimal time off rather than any period of extended leave.

That said, there is absolutely no right or wrong here. The point is, it's up to you to decide what feels right for you. And then make that clear. Believe me, your manager will be grateful for the information.

I didn't get an invite to the Christmas party and felt really left out.

(Parent-on-leave, getting ready to return)

When you're contacted

What about the when? It's worth considering if there are any timeframes around this. For example, if you're planning to take nine months off, do you want to protect your first few months and ask that contact is purely initiated by you (major news aside)? Do you only want the big client/team news in the few months before you come back or throughout?

How you're contacted

The final piece is the 'how'. Would you like all contact to come from your manager or would you like to have someone in the team to be your eyes and ears? A friend, perhaps? Or a mixture of both? A friend for the social stuff/team get-togethers and your manager for major news? Do you want to keep receiving regular team updates by email etc.? What about any external contacts? Do you want to stay in touch with them directly? Do you need to make sure your manager is kept in the loop if you do?

Of course, every organization and team is different – and so are you – but it's really helpful to think about what you want and then share that.

☐ **Think about your return and consider discussing any flexibility requirements before you go**

In the same way as talking about whether you might like to use KIT days before you start your leave, it can be really helpful to have a conversation around flexibility. If only brief. I was fortunate in that my manager brought it up. They made it clear what they would be open to and what they would find harder. I'll be honest, in that moment I didn't love everything they said! I did, however, really appreciate them approaching the subject and, later on, I realized just how helpful it had been to discuss it then.

Why? Firstly, because it gave me time to absorb it. Frankly, at that stage my only thoughts had been that I might be interested in coming back to work less than five days a week. I hadn't given a lot of thought to what a future working pattern might look like. I had always worked full time, so I found it hard to get my head around another way of working. And more than that, I was very focused on my imminent arrival rather than my return.

The second reason I think it's so valuable to start exploring this now is because of what I've just said. You're likely not to be giving it a huge amount of thought yet and neither is anyone else – so the pressure is off. You can start having exploratory conversations without anyone – you included – feeling committed to anything you're discussing. It's purely research. Talk to other parents; see what they've found works for them. If they're on your team, so much the better, but at any rate if you know (or can get to know) other parents working flexibly in your company, ask them about their experiences. If any of their models appeal, and your manager has yet to open the conversation, I highly recommend opening it yourself.

It's also worth finding out if your employer, or your country, has any specific policies or benefits around this. A small but increasing number of employers are offering part-time return for full-time pay (e.g. Vodafone[8]) or have formal ramp-up policies in place (like Airbnb[9]). The same is true for countries. In Belgium, for example, you may be entitled to up to four months of paid leave, which can either be taken in a block (e.g. to extend parental leave) or to enable a part-time return for full-time pay.[10] And in Germany you can return and work up to 32 hours per week and still claim parental allowance for the hours you aren't currently working (if you have any allowance left at this point).[11]

And please, if you're thinking 'this doesn't apply to me' – it does. Even if you're planning to come back to your role on exactly the same terms. As a parent you are guaranteed to need some level of flexibility. It doesn't have to be the formal X days a week/different hours. It may just be informal. You will need it and there are lots of ways to make it work; the sooner you start thinking about it, the more chance you have of making it work really well for you, and your organization.

☐ Make a list of key stakeholders

Before you head off it can be really useful to spend a few minutes writing a list of your key stakeholders – clients, suppliers, press, industry contacts and, if you're in a large organization, your internal network too. Decide who you want to stay in touch with/ keep informed about what, both before you go and while you're on leave (although I'd recommend not overburdening yourself with the latter). And then perhaps most useful of all you'll have a list to refer to when you get back and to help you re-integrate more quickly.

☐ Make a note of key systems/logins

A small thing, but it can reduce the headache on your return! Some of them will change anyway, but making a list of the key systems you use, the current usernames and (security considerations permitting) passwords can help you get back up and running more quickly.

☐ Reflect on your achievements

Consider taking some time to reflect on what you've achieved, the skills you've developed, what you're getting really good at. The experience you have under your belt, what's unique to you. It can be all too easy to forget this when you're on leave and, to be honest, even before you go. We don't often take the time to look at this holistically. We might have a success here and there but thinking of it as a whole is really confidence boosting.

And that's what this is about. You want your confidence to be as high as possible when you go on leave. Because being on extended leave can sap your confidence. Most of us are all too good at focusing on the negatives and forgetting the positives. This exercise will not only give you a boost in the moment but, if you write it down, it can prove even more valuable later on. When you're maybe feeling a bit low.

What's the best way to go about this? It doesn't have to be a mammoth exercise. Just ask yourself some simple questions and see what answers you get. Here's a few to get you started:

- What are you most proud of?
- What have you done that has had the most impact?
- What are you really good at?
- How have you grown professionally?
- Where have you surprised yourself?
- Who have you helped most and how?
- What are you the go-to person for?
- How would those you know admire you describe you?
- What have you noticed or realized you're better at than you thought?

And in terms of timeframe, I would encourage you to think both in terms of your career as a whole and the time since you last had any kind of formal performance review.

☐ Arrange a meeting to discuss your performance and aspirations

Just like the annual leave year, the chances are your child's arrival will not be in sync with your next major performance review. You might be thinking, so what? Or even, it's a relief to miss one! Or maybe your organization doesn't even have a regular review cycle. Whatever the situation, I would strongly encourage you to at the very least consider having a conversation with your manager before you go. As a way to bookend the time before you went on leave. To look back at the progress you've made. Those achievements we've just talked about. And to discuss your aspirations going forward.

Not only will this help you both recognize your contribution, it will also help avoid any assumptions being made. You can tell this is a theme for me. It's all too easy for assumptions to be made about the wishes of those not there. Out of sight, out of mind? If you're on leave when there's a team restructure, or an opportunity for promotion or even a sideways move you might have been interested in, if your manager isn't aware, they could all too easily assume you wouldn't be interested.

Again, I feel it's important to say there is absolutely no right or wrong here. You may feel you want to go on leave, see how you feel when you get back and that just adapting will be a big challenge (and it is). But if you're keen to keep progressing there's nothing wrong with that either. Be clear about what you do and don't want.

And if you're not sure, tell them that too. Again, your manager will be grateful, and your wishes will be front of mind when it matters.

☐ Think about your first week back in the organization

Think about the people you'll want to reconnect with (perhaps using your list of key stakeholders). The systems you use regularly (and login details/passwords – they may change but it might prove a helpful reminder). The regular processes you need to be familiar with. It will be an invaluable reference point for those first weeks back and help you to get back in the saddle more quickly.

☐ Consider how long you expect to be off – and if you're comfortable sharing this

Again, this is very personal and there is no right or wrong. Not only might you change your mind, but there are usually timeframes in place to support this – in the UK for example, you don't have to confirm this until eight weeks before you return. So why am I suggesting thinking about it now? Firstly, in my experience, most people have a general idea of when they want to come back. They've done any maths on the financial implications, know how keen they are to resume their career and so have a sense of how much time they're likely to be off. Secondly, it's a very helpful piece of information to share. As I've said, you're not bound to it, but it helps enormously with planning.

Think about it from your manager's perspective for a moment. They have a valued team member going on leave for months. It might be three months. It might be 12. If you're in Germany, you may even be considering taking the full three years. That's a big difference. It could make a huge difference to how your role is covered. And perhaps most importantly for you, if they have an idea of when you're thinking of coming back, they know when to factor you in. Especially if in X months' time there are changes afoot. If they know you're considering coming back in the next few months and have expressed interest in a change in role… you can see where I'm going. Helping them helps you. And to reiterate – you are not tied to this so I can only see upside in giving an indication – and if you're wondering how to phrase this without it being a commitment, just say something along the lines of 'I'm thinking I'll probably take X months off and so be back around Y (whatever date that is), but I'm not really sure how I'll feel so I'll let you know if that changes'. It really will be appreciated.

And if you're looking at this from a manager's perspective and wanting to open this conversation, without putting pressure on, talking about what contact someone wants is a great way to do this. 'Have you thought about what contact you do and don't want while you're on leave?' 'Do you want to reach out to me when you're ready to talk about your return/if you're interested in doing some KIT days?' 'Would it be helpful for me to make a note in the diary and check in with you?' All very sensible questions that open the door to a conversation around return timelines without putting on any pressure.

Doing some preparation – at home

It's not just work where you can do some preparation. There are some things to think about on the home front too.

☐ Think about your childcare options and start exploring them

Yes, now. It may seem early, and if you're lucky it may be very straightforward, but for most people it's a little more complicated than they expect. Like me, you may not even have a strong view at this stage of what you want – or even what all the options actually are. And you may not have considered if you want one type of childcare or a combination. Plus, if you're considering returning to a different working pattern that makes things even more complicated.

But before we get ahead of ourselves, I'm not suggesting you should be working all of this out now; I'm just saying start to research your options. Thinking about what appeals to you and might work for you as a family. For example, if nursery is an option, go and look at local ones. You don't have to commit, but the process will help you become clearer on what you need and, importantly perhaps, what feels right.

You may also find popular nurseries have long waiting lists which only require a small deposit to join, so if they're on your short list you might want to sign up. This is true in many countries. Kita (childcare in Germany), for example, has become particularly competitive in larger cities. Equally, there is only an upside in starting to build a relationship with a childminder you like.

And it's well worth exploring any financial support available in your country to help towards the cost of childcare such as the **Tax-Free Childcare** scheme in the UK.

Explainer: Childcare options

To help you get started, here's a quick run through of the various options for paid childcare in the UK.

Childminders – care for children within the childminder's own home, sometimes alongside their own children.

Day nurseries – care for children until they are old enough to go to school (some organizations offer these on site to their employees).

Nannies – a nanny is someone who is employed to look after a child or children in their own home. Sometimes they live in and sometimes two families will have a 'nanny share' to either keep a nanny occupied full time by splitting the week, or by having the children together to help reduce the cost and provide more interaction with other little ones for their children.

Au pairs – these are generally young people or students from another country, who help with childcare and/or housework while learning the language. It's normal for the family to provide them with a room, food and some pocket money.

☐ Consider which family and friends could help

I've listed this separately because family and friends may form not just part of your formal childcare arrangement while you're working but also help with babysitting and perhaps give you some support while you're still on leave and be the first people you and your partner trust with your child in your absence. It's also a different type of conversation because it's personal, not professional, regardless of whether you agree to compensate them in some way.

It's very easy to make assumptions – on both sides. Having open and honest conversations is crucial. Grandparents, many of whom may want to be involved, are often a first port of call. The big question is: how much do they want to commit and how much do you want them involved? There is a world of difference between helping out on an ad hoc basis and becoming part of the childcare you rely on for your weekly routine. Whether grandparents live locally or not may make some of this decision for you. It's also important to think about what's realistic at their age. It's incredibly exhausting looking after a little one, especially a young baby.

Getting really clear on what it is what you need and what help, if any, you want from them is the first step.

☐ Start thinking about the kind of parent you want to be

There are entire books dedicated to this subject and it's not my intention to even scratch the surface of this vast subject, but it is definitely a good time to take a moment to start thinking about this. Before you dive in. And talk to your partner, if you have one, while there is no pressure.

I am sure most parents would agree, parenting is probably the ultimate 'learning on the job' role you will ever have. And you will make mistakes. Without a doubt. We all do. Sometimes it feels like on a daily basis! That's not meant to frighten you. The opposite, in fact. You are human. But having an overall vision of what you want your family life to look like can be really helpful. Something to guide you in harder moments. So, if this appeals, do a little light reading on the subject and talk to friends/family with children about their approach and what works. A word of warning, though: everyone (and I mean *everyone*) will have strong views on this. So, whilst for some (and I am one of those), talking it through will help enormously, for others it does not (and that may include your partner). Most of all, remember this is about what feels right *for you and your family*.

Key takeaways from this chapter

- Use your checklist to help you get a sense of where you need to focus your efforts
- Get clear on the practical stuff – pay, benefits and relevant policies
- Reflect on your achievements and discuss your aspirations
- Think about what you want – sharing your news, arranging cover, whether to ramp down
- Think ahead – about how you're contacted when you're on leave, the flexibility you might need and childcare options, while there's no pressure
- Start preparing for your return – yes, now!

If you're supporting your partner/someone close to you

Encourage them to be proactive and think about their return before they go on leave; help them think through the options. Start thinking about how you'll make this work both as a family and in your own role as a working parent.

What flexibility might you need? What's going to change for you when your partner is returning to work and what conversations could you have now that will make that easier?

If you're supporting someone in your team

Set the tone from the start. Position yourself as someone who is there to help them get the answers to their questions. Get informed – make sure you're up to speed on pay, benefits and relevant policies. Talk to them – about sharing their news, arranging cover, whether to ramp down and if/how they want to stay in touch. And keep talking to them – check in regularly to make sure they're ok, discuss their aspirations and don't make assumptions. Finally, start thinking ahead – what might their return look like? What type of flexibility do you think they might need and what are you comfortable talking to them about on now? They are guaranteed to be really grateful to you for opening this conversation…

Reflections on Part 1

As we come to the end of Part 1, it's worth taking a moment to reflect on the challenges and digest some of the ideas to overcome them. How are you feeling about your own parental leave? Have your concerns changed since you started reading? Are you feeling more concerned about some things than you were and less about others?

Exercise 3.1: What are your takeaways from Part 1?

What are your key outstanding concerns?	Who could help? What actions could you take?

Part 2

While you're away on parental leave

Chapter 4

Reviewing what has and hasn't changed

Being on leave with a new child, especially a young baby, is at times all-consuming, particularly in the early days. For many of us it's one of the most wonderful and at the same time exhausting periods we have ever experienced. Work can feel like a different lifetime. At some point, though, the thought of returning will seep back into your mind and thereafter with increasing urgency. Some people feel very excited at the prospect. For others, it's something they find themselves wanting to put off. Or you may find yourself swinging from one to the other – I know I did! But one thing most people have in common is, it can feel daunting. That's ok. There's a lot to think about.

In this chapter, we start by exploring what's often front of mind when you think about your return to work and then unpick what's most important to you.

What's front of mind as you think about returning?

There is arguably a long list of things to think about when you're planning your return. Let's start at the high level with some common themes...

1. Practical

For many, their first focus when they start thinking about going back to work is the practical side. For most people there's already been a big change to everyday logistics to manage and you're likely very conscious this is only going to increase on your return. There is of course the big one: getting the right childcare in place. But there are lots of other pieces to the puzzle. Agreeing a **return date**. Negotiating any changes to days/hours. Agreeing with your partner/anyone else supporting you who will do what in terms of drop-offs, pick-ups etc. Factoring in potential KIT days. Using **accrued annual leave**. Ramping up or just jumping back in. It can feel like an endless to-do list. But one with a very big emotional backpack attached to it.

2. Emotional

Then there's the emotional side. Having another human being totally dependent on you is life-changing. Getting yourself comfortable with leaving your new child in the care of another takes time. For some more than others. The guilt starts to creep in. The effects of lack of sleep don't help. Nor does the extended period away from the workplace. Even the most self-assured parents can experience a drop in confidence or, at the very least, a wobble or two.

3. Aspirational

Finally, there's how you feel about your career progression to factor in. Having a child may have changed your ambitions, one way or the other. Or it may not have changed them at all. It may also have impacted the perspectives of those in a position to influence your career. Are you still going to get that promised promotion? Or do you just want to spend some time getting used to working alongside looking after your new child before you even think about the next step? More questions to be answered. Have a go at Exercise 4.1 and see if that helps to make things clearer.

Exercise 4.1: How are you feeling about your return right now?

Before we get too far into this, as in Chapter 1, take a moment to think about how you are feeling about returning today – right now – and note it down. There are no right or wrong answers here. In the same way as every pregnancy is unique, so is everyone's experience of parental leave. It follows, then, that how you will feel about returning to work will also be unique. And this is likely to change over time.

Try not to refer back to your notes/answers from Chapter 1 at this point, or at least not before you've jotted down your immediate thoughts! If you do look back afterwards, you'll probably notice a shift in priorities. Some of your early concerns have probably reduced and new ones will have crept in to take their place.

For now, though, I want you to ask yourself the following questions and write down the first thoughts that come to mind. Be really honest with yourself. No one else is going to read this list unless you choose to share it with them. And no concern is too small. If it's bothering you, write it down. And again, consider involving a partner or friend and look at this as a living list that grows with you. Revisit it as often as you like as you progress through the book.

What have you already noticed you're feeling differently about now to before you went on leave?

What are your biggest concerns when you think about returning to work?

What are you feeling really positive or sure about?

Once you've done this, take a moment to process what's on your mind. Are there any themes emerging? For example, it could be you can't see how you're going to manage drop-off and pick-up with your commute, or that you feel very nervous about leaving your child or re-joining your team – or all of these and more! That's okay. As ever, being aware of what's worrying you is half the battle. Take some time to recognize what you're feeling good about. And why that might be. It could be as simple as having some adult conversation and the chance to drink an entire hot drink without interruption!

Re-read and let it sink in...

The top 10 most common concerns at this point

Now you've spent some time thinking about what's front of mind for you, you're probably wondering if these are the same concerns as those of others. Here's a summary of the 10 most common concerns I have heard expressed at this point. You'll probably recognize some crossover with the list in Chapter 1 but note the concerns are likely to be more specific at this point and new ones have appeared. Also note there is no order of importance here and you may experience all of these at one point or another, or you may find yourself very focused on a few.

1. Lack of clarity over your options for return

A lot of people find they have been so focused on leaving work and their new arrival that their return is something they find they have pushed to the back of their mind. You may not be totally clear on what your options are. This can be made harder if you're not sure who to speak to. Perhaps you have a new manager. Or think you should start with your people team. You may be aware of KIT days, but no one has mentioned using them and you're not sure how these fit in with using accrued annual leave. Or whether your return date is fixed or can be moved. Things get even more complicated if you and your partner are sharing your leave.

2. Apprehension over agreeing a new working arrangement

Your views about what you ideally want your working life to look like will probably have evolved since you first found out you were expecting a child. You may have a very clear idea of what you'd like and are worried about how that will be received by your employer.

Perhaps you think they will say no. Or you may have a less fixed view and just not have any real idea of how to approach the conversation or what the timelines are. This is very common and the source of a great deal of anxiety. Particularly when you factor in agreeing your working pattern has a big impact on your childcare arrangements (and vice versa).

It may surprise you to learn that this is also the source of a great deal of anxiety for managers. I hear questions like 'Can I say "No"?' and encouragingly, increasingly, 'How do I say "Yes"?' Uncertainty is no one's friend. And this particular challenge can feel like a minefield you have to tiptoe across for all involved.

3. Feeling behind/out of the loop

Being out of the organization for an extended period of time can be really tough. Especially if you have had little contact while you've been out. You can find yourself feeling out of the loop. Not up to speed with the latest priorities of the organization/your team. Maybe feeling a bit behind skills wise, particularly if you have a technical role. Even feeling you're not part of the team the way you were before. This can be very unsettling. It can make you feel very much on the back foot. Maybe that your chances of that promotion are further away. Or simply feeling the need to prove yourself again.

4. Feeling you won't be able to do the work in the same way as before

A lot of people are concerned that their new role as a parent will impact their ability to do their job. This could be linked to practicalities such as a long commute. Or that the new boundaries you think you'll have to work within will mean you can no longer so freely go in early or work late. Perhaps you're concerned about the social side. About it being difficult to go along to team events in the future, and what this might mean for your career. And then, of course, there's the big one: guilt. Guilt that you won't be working the same hours as before and so maybe won't be able to get as much done as before you became a parent.

5. How you'll juggle work and home

Again, a very common concern. I think every working parent wonders how they will make it work! And on a regular basis. Deep breath. Lack of sleep again is an enemy here. There are also very real differences to factor in. Your workload, which for many is a serious concern when they think about returning. How you'll juggle work with pick-up and drop-off, particularly if you opt for a nursery with strict hours and fines for lateness. How you'll find time for yourself (exercise, seeing your friends) or your relationship (vs feeling like a tag team and ships that pass in the night). Another big influencer can be family support or a lack of it. Not having family nearby to help can be a major cause of worry. Having no one to be your back up, your Plan B.

6. Concern about whether you have the right childcare in place

This is a biggie. Probably the one every parent wrestles over. Working out what childcare you need in terms of days/hours. The type of childcare you want – nanny, nursery, childminder, family or a combination thereof. What you can afford. If it's right for your child. How you will know. What you will do if it's not working. And then there's the additional dimension of family support. You may feel you need to accept an offer of help for financial reasons. Even if you're really happy to accept the help, you may still have reservations over how much influence this person will have on your child. How you can in turn set boundaries and manage expectations.

7. Anxiety over leaving your child and guilt

Yes, guilt again. I don't think I have ever spoken to a parent who hasn't mentioned guilt at some point. Whether it's guilt at not doing a good enough job at work, or guilt at not doing a good enough job at home. Usually both... it's natural and almost inevitable.

Many find it incredibly hard to leave their child in the care of someone else. Their child, who they've been with almost 24/7 in the last however many months. What if something happens to them when you're not there? It can feel a terrifying prospect. If you're reading this while you're still expecting, or perhaps just to get a better understanding of the challenges, that may sound hard to get your head around. But even now as a parent of a school-age child I still experience this on a regular basis, albeit to a lesser extent (just to reassure you).

Then there's guilt about looking forward to being at work and away from your child. There. I said it. Not everyone feels like this but most of us at least have moments (me included). The thought of being able to have an entire cup of tea/coffee or adult conversation without interruption! Or just go to the loo in peace. I remember someone in a workshop looking visibly relieved to admit they were excited about returning to work and how guilty they had been feeling about it!

I feel guilty about not feeling guilty about returning to work!

(Mum-on-leave, about to return)

8. Concern about your workplace being set up for your return

This one is specifically for those who plan on breastfeeding once they are back at work. Depending on the type of role you have and how well your employer is set up, this may be a bigger or smaller issue. Many employers have focused on this in recent years (or are now) and have hugely improved both the facilities available and the awareness of the wider teams to be sensitive to this need, in the same way as they are in allowing for prayer time, for example. That doesn't mean it won't be something you aren't concerned about. It's new to you, after all, and you may not be one of the lucky ones with a more enlightened employer. Add to this, for most people, it's a very personal thing to have to find time for in the workplace and can feel strange and out of context. And as one parent recently told me, 'It's hard to remember to do', which can be stressful in itself.

It's hard to remember to do [pump].

(Recently returned mum, still breastfeeding)

9. Isolation

Being the only parent in your team can be hard. It can make you feel very different. If you know you're going back into that environment it can feel daunting. You may be worried about being left out. You may feel it has already happened while you've been on leave. Being at home looking after a little one can be isolating in itself. Not everyone wants to go to all the various classes. And whilst meeting up with other new parents can be a real lifeline, you can feel you just want to have a conversation about something other than children! But if your friends/team are not parents, they may not fill that need, as you find yourself feeling they just don't get it.

10. Your career stalling

An increasing number of people I speak to are concerned about the impact on their career of having a period out. Often, they were on track for a promotion before they went on leave and are worried things may have changed in their absence. This can be particularly acute when there's been a change in manager. Questions like 'Will I have to prove myself again?' can seep into your mind. It can be very demotivating.

Your motivations for returning

This previous point about your career stalling makes for a nice segue to an important and sometimes forgotten point: your motivation for returning. It's a big change, so it's well worth being really clear about why you're making it.

You may be reading this and thinking it's pretty black and white: I need to earn money. And maybe it is. But in my experience that isn't the only reason people return to work after having a child. And for most people, particularly given the cost of childcare, it's not as straightforward as it may sound on the surface.

Of course, there are family finances to consider. 'It's just not worth me going back to work' is a phrase that I always find hard to hear. It's totally understandable to consider the impact of childcare costs against the returning parents salary – and it's a very real issue in countries where childcare costs are high, like the UK – but it's not the only consideration. There are lots of other reasons to return. You love your job. Your longer term career progression (and income). You value the independence. The mental stimulation. The connection to others. It gives you a sense of identity beyond being a parent and partner. And it makes you a better parent.

All of this certainly played a part for me. There were times when I found it tough being at home with a small baby. The routine of it. The lack of mental stimulation. It's actually hard for me to admit that. And I am a little worried about my daughter one day reading this and being hurt by it. I think there's a part of us that feels we should all totally love being on parental leave. Don't get me wrong, there were a lot of parts I loved and I wouldn't have missed it for the world, but for me coming back was about more than the money. And I do think I'm a better parent for having continued to work alongside being a parent.

How you feel may be similar. Or it may be very different. There's no judgement here. The point is to take a moment to think about your own motivations. Be honest with yourself about what's driving your decision. It can really help to have this in your mind when you're building your return plan. When you're having those conversations that will shape your working life going forward.

Exercise 4.2: What's motivating you to return?

Having read the section on motivation, take a moment to consider your motivations for returning to work. You can use the following grid if you find it helpful, but this is not exhaustive so don't be restricted by it (hence the spare rows). I have found it helpful to consider their relative importance too. What are the main drivers and what are secondary?

What's motivating your return?

	Hugely important	Important	A factor	Not a factor at all
Income/security (short and long term)				
Love what you do				
Sense of identity				
Mental stimulation				
Connection/ adult conversation/ part of team				
Independence/ freedom				
Important for your confidence				

Your career aspirations

Your motivations can also impact on your career aspirations. You may find these are different now to what they were before you went on leave.

I made a very conscious decision to return to work. Yes, earning was a factor, but if I had felt really strongly about not working, we could have juggled things financially. It would have taken some adjustments, but we could have done it. That made me very conscious of my job delivering what I wanted from it. What I needed. To feel valued and that I was making a contribution. To be continually learning and stretching myself mentally.

I found this surprisingly empowering. And different from how I looked at work before I had my daughter. If I was going to pay someone else to look after her, I wanted that to be a good trade. To be both of benefit to me and my daughter/our family. If anything, I became more ambitious. I valued my time more and so was smarter with how I used it. More on that later (see Chapter 9).

This doesn't mean I went back on full throttle asking for a promotion on Day 1 (although I'm not saying you shouldn't, either!); I'm just trying to make the point that I felt differently and it's worth exploring if you feel differently and if so, how. So, you can consider what that might mean for you.

Exercise 4.3: What are your aspirations right now?

Being honest with yourself about your career aspirations and whether these have changed since before you went on leave is really important. For you and for those around you.

What are your career aspirations now? Do you want to progress and, if so, what does that mean in terms of your role and in what timeframe?

How important to you is having time to adjust? What does that look like to you and what timeframe do you ideally want to work to? What impact, if any, does this have on your career aspirations?

Keep revisiting this – as you've probably guessed, how you feel about this is likely to change over time.

Revisit your list

As we wrap up this chapter, I'd also like to encourage you to take another look at the list of concerns you may have had at the start. Has reading this chapter uncovered any other questions or challenges in your mind? Do note them down if it has, so you can refer back to them again later and make sure we've tackled them all.

Key takeaways from this chapter

- Be aware of what's front of mind for you as you start thinking about returning to work
- Consider the impact these may have on your mindset
- Think through your motivations for returning to work
- Think about your career aspirations and if they have changed, even in the short-term – or not

If you're supporting your partner/someone close to you

Talk to them about their concerns and try and help them work out which ones they can address now, and how. Are there any you can help them work through, like arranging childcare and balancing this with both of you working? Is their decision to return based just on finances today or are you looking at all the reasons to return?

If you're supporting someone in your team

Make sure you don't forget about them while they're on leave and be aware of what might be front of mind as they start thinking about their return. What might be most important for them and how could you help? Are you making any assumptions? What were their aspirations before they went on leave? Do you have any evidence this might have changed?

Chapter 5

Preparing for conversations with managers, colleagues and key stakeholders

Planning your return is not something you can do in isolation. It will involve lots of conversations, both at home and at work. How do you make sure these go smoothly and you get the right outcome, for you and the organization? In this chapter we'll explore the key steps, the conversations you'll need to have and what to consider before you do.

Let's start with the key steps. For most people, they will look a bit like this:

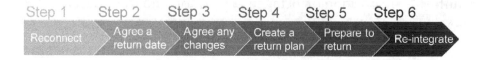

I say for most people, as you may feel you don't need to reconnect because you've stayed in regular contact with your team, or you may not have changed your mind on your return date and so on. At a minimum, though, you still need to reconfirm this and it's worth walking through each step and sense checking before moving on.

For the purposes of this chapter, we will concentrate on the first four steps, starting with reconnecting.

Step 1: Reconnecting

To have any meaningful conversations with your manager about your return you need to be back in touch. If you've been in regular touch throughout your leave, your manager is the same and you have a good relationship with them, this may be very straightforward. You might call/email/message them to say you're keen to catch up and arrange to meet them. The harder work here, then, is preparing for that meeting: Step 2 onwards. (And before you jump straight to Step 2 if this applies to you, do look at the last two paragraphs here on 'when to reach out'.)

However, not everyone has it that easy. Some people find they have a different manager, or they simply haven't been in touch since they left, so this first step feels like a big one. So, let's break it down into smaller steps...

Who to speak to

First off, who do you need to speak to? Your starting point is your manager, even if they are new to you. And if you're in the unfortunate position of being in any doubt who they are, either ask your previous manager (if they're still in the organization) or ask for help from your people team. And yes, this really does happen. I've spoken to people in that position who literally didn't even know who to speak to. 'I think I have a new manager but I'm not sure who they are.' It's more common than you might think, particularly in larger organizations who tend to regularly restructure, but it can happen in smaller organizations too. In an ideal world they should have informed you, but there can be good reasons why this hasn't happened or just hasn't happened yet.

I think I have a new manager but I'm not sure who they are.

(Parent-on-leave, about to return to work)

And if for whatever reason this feels daunting, and you have a good relationship with someone in the people team, they could also be a great first step, but you will need to talk to your manager at some point soon.

How to get in touch

Once you work out who to speak to, think about how you contact them. This is totally up to you, and I don't want to teach anyone to suck eggs here, but I'm also aware for some people this is a big step. An email is probably best if you haven't spoken for a while, or they are new to you. Keep it brief at this stage and resist the temptation to hit them with everything at once! Far better to make the aim of this simply to make contact and arrange a time to talk properly, ideally in person or if that's not practical a call – video if you can. I say that because it's in your interests to start to build/ rebuild a relationship with them and it's easier to do that in person or if they can see your face.

When to reach out

The other thing to think about here is timing. When to reconnect. This slightly depends on what you're trying to achieve. If it's simply to reconfirm a date you have both already pencilled in it's more straightforward and all you need to do is to make sure you do this within the relevant timeframe – eight weeks before you're due to return in the UK.

If, however, you're either looking to change the date you return or to discuss some change in your working arrangement you're going to need longer. Factoring this in when you're judging when to reach out can take off some of the pressure, which is a good thing on both sides. As a general rule, I would say allow at least a month for these kind of discussions before your deadline to confirm (don't forget you've got diaries to think about as well) – so for those in the UK, you want to start discussions three months before you return. That said, there's no reason not to do this earlier, particularly if you're juggling confirming your childcare arrangements and need certainty around your plans sooner.

Step 2: Agreeing a return date

So, you've arranged a meeting with your manager to talk about your return. The first thing to get clear on is the date you want to return. When you went on leave you were likely aware of the maximum amount of time you could take off and what the financial implications were for you, depending on your own circumstances and the extra support from your employer (if any). You may also have had an idea in your head of how long you were going to take off. You may have shared this with your employer, or you may not. And you are allowed to change your mind.

If you're sharing leave this may be more concrete if you've agreed a plan with your partner and you're factoring in their employer as well. It may also feel like something dictated by law. For some people, though, it can feel less set in stone. For most of us it's a bit of both.

What do I mean by that? Well, yes, there is a limit on the amount of time you can take as parental leave… that is set in law. But there is some flexibility when applying this to your return date.

Changing your return date

So, in theory in most situations there is an opportunity to adjust your return by a little or even a lot. Let's take a standard UK maternity leave as an example. Unless you've told them otherwise, your employer is likely to assume you will be back 52 weeks after you started your leave. They will pencil this into their HR systems. From your point of view, if you want this to be any different (for example, you want to return before the 52 weeks) you need to let them know, and, as mentioned earlier, by law you need to give them at least eight weeks' notice.[1] So that they can be ready. They may have taken on someone to do your role in your absence who either needs to leave or be transferred to another position. On the flip side, there is often also the option to extend the time you're not actually back by a small amount, using your annual leave (see Step 4).

Think about what would work for you so you're ready to discuss it with your manager. For example, if you went on maternity just before Christmas you might want to agree a return in the New Year. Or you may want to make sure you're back in time for the annual team strategy day/offsite. They may prefer this as well. You may have indicated you'd return after nine months and have decided you want to take an extra couple of months. There is a lot of flexibility here.

Just to reiterate, how much time you take off is totally personal and totally up to you. The one thing that is universal, though, is it can be really helpful if no one (not you or your manager) feels under pressure on this, so give yourselves (and them) plenty of time to agree this. Getting clarity on your return date is important for you in many ways, not least your own peace of mind and in finalizing your childcare arrangements, so it's worth getting it right.

Step 3: Agreeing any changes to your working arrangement

For some people this is straightforward. They are returning to exactly the same role. The same hours, the same location, even the same manager. But for many, at least one of these may have changed. Some things will change that are outside of your control. A manager leaving or moving onto to a new role, perhaps a restructure that means a change in role you. Other changes will be those you are looking to make. A change in your hours and/or the days you work, or a preference for working more (or, in some cases, less) from home. If you work on client sites (which is the case in many jobs from consulting to construction), it may be that you want to make sure your first project is not too far from home so you can limit your commute. The list goes on.

Let's start with the changes outside of your control. If there have been big changes to your team or reporting line, hopefully you have been kept in the loop. I say 'hopefully', as I'm very aware this isn't always the case, as we saw earlier. It's not a great place to start and can make you feel very much on the back foot, but it's normally a reflection of either oversight or good intentions, albeit potentially misplaced in my opinion, such as not wanting to intrude on your leave. If there have been changes to your role you should already be aware, regardless of whether you're on parental leave or not.

If you're already aware of this, it's likely top of your agenda for your meeting. To find out what has changed since you left and what this might mean for you and your role. And remember, it's not always bad news, there could be an opportunity to accept a promotion or secure a new role and expand your skills.

What about changes within your control? Let's start with your role. You may have told your manager before you went on leave that you'd be interested in new roles, as we talked about earlier. Or it may be something you want to discuss with them now. You may have thought you would just want to go back to the same role, but you may be feeling differently now. The key thing here is to be really clear with what you want so you avoid assumptions being made.

That doesn't mean they won't be. One solo parent shared a not-so-good story with me. Their organization had expanded globally, and they expressed their interest in a 'group role' that would involve travel. The reaction they got was along the lines of 'you're on your own with a child, how can you travel?' – as if they hadn't even considered that and have a plan. As they said, 'very frustrating and insulting'. This story didn't have a great ending – it left the parent with a bitter taste in their mouth, and they quickly moved on to another role within the wider business, so a loss for that team. But if you're clear in sharing your aspirations, you at least reduce the chance of these kind of situations and, if nothing else, at least you will have done all you can and have no regrets. And in many cases, managers will listen and be delighted at you initiating this and knowing what you're open to, as well as what you're not.

Now let's take a look at changes you'd like to make to your working pattern, your days, hours etc. If this is something you think you want, it can feel daunting. It might be you fear your employer won't react well. Or you're concerned about the impact on your career progression. Or simply you just don't know how to go about asking.

Let's break it down again. Firstly, as mentioned in Part 1 (see Chapter 3) an increasing number of both countries and organizations are enhancing the provisions for working parents to work more flexibly (as well as employees more generally), so find out if there is anything relevant for you.

What about if there isn't? I'd like to share a little about my experience of this. I planned to take nine months' maternity leave and give or take a week I did. So far so good. My role was still there, and my maternity cover (who has since become a great friend) was taking a permanent role as the team grew. Another tick. My manager was the same. Great. I did, however, want to change the hours I worked or, more specifically, the number of days.

You may recall, I mentioned in Part 1 (see Chapter 3) that I had had a conversation with my manager before I went on leave around what might be acceptable in terms of flexibility. For me this was crucial. As I mentioned, I wasn't especially happy with what they said at the time (and I hope if they are reading this they are smiling and will read on!) but it gave me time to take on board what they had said, which turned out to be really important.

What happened? I was interested in exploring working part time instead of five days. They made it clear they were very open to four days; three days might be harder. However, and this was the big one for me, they were not keen on me taking either a Monday or a Friday off. I remember feeling a little surprised and, if I'm honest, irritated by this at the time. As far as I saw it, everyone who worked part time got a long weekend, so why shouldn't I?

To be fair, to them and me, I listened to their logic, and it was difficult to argue with. Mondays were when our team meetings were. As an internal consultancy team, we worked with senior stakeholders across the organization, which meant we often sat physically with the teams we were working with for most of the week, and it was therefore even more important to have that team time. Fair point. What about Fridays? Because of that high level of involvement with senior stakeholders, they also felt being out Fridays would prove challenging if those internal clients were trying to reach me late on a Thursday or Friday morning and wouldn't get a response until Monday. This felt weaker to me, but I could relate to it.

More interesting potentially is less the detail here, or frankly my opinions of it, but what the outcome was. They encouraged me to consider taking a Wednesday off instead. When I considered what it was that I really wanted, I realized the 'long weekend' wasn't important at all. It was just what I saw as the norm and so had jumped to the conclusion this was the obvious answer. I realized what I wanted was quality time with my daughter. I also realized I really enjoyed the vibe in the office on a Friday and didn't want to miss out on that. Suddenly Wednesdays off looked more like not just a serious option but an attractive one.

Having had that conversation before I went on leave made having this conversation so much easier. I had had time to weigh up the pros and cons. What was driving my desire to change to four days. What I really needed from it – and what I didn't.

And in case you're wondering how it panned out, once I started working this pattern, I found I absolutely loved it. I loved having a dedicated day with my daughter that didn't get swallowed up by the weekend. I loved only ever having two days away from her. I loved what I came to see as my mid-week weekend. Not just for me, but for my work. Just the same way you find yourself mulling problems you have on a Friday over a weekend (or equivalent if you work a different pattern) and sometimes what feels like miraculously you have resolved them in the back of your mind by Monday, the same happened for me. I arguably became better at my job as a result. As well as happy with the balance I had. The most important thing to take from this story? I found what was right for me at that point AND what would work well for the organization.

OK, so how do we break this down? Let's take a look at the thinking you need to do first and then how to set yourself up for the best possible conversation on this.

Before you discuss it/submit a request

Before you have a conversation, you need to be really clear what it is you want, what's driving that and what options you might have.

1. Think long and hard about what you actually want

What are your objectives? Does it have to be specific days you have off? Or hours that you work? Are you (like I did) jumping to conclusions? Are you feeling under pressure to clarify childcare arrangements?

Side note here: be aware, because a lot of people who work part time are off on Fridays (and to a lesser extent Mondays), these can often be the quietest days and so you may give yourself more options if you choose to work these days. You may even get a better rate at some childcare providers. Equally, you may be trying to work around the commitments of extended family members who are helping, or your partners work commitments as well as your own. Some of these may be very fixed, but it's worth sense checking and making sure you're not making assumptions that will limit your options before you start.

2. Consider if it's a formal or informal arrangement you need

There are pros and cons to both. In the UK, if you're looking to change from full time to part time it will involve a formal contract change – which you have no right to revert without mutual agreement. That was a bit of a moment for me, it felt very final! This is not the case everywhere, Germany being a prime example, as referenced earlier. Of course, in reality it was no different to when you change jobs and agree new terms and conditions. If, on the other hand, you just need some flexibility over your start or finish time, depending on your role you may not need to make this official. It may be something you can simply agree with your manager. This is probably truer now than it was even five years ago. Many more organizations are adopting hybrid models and focusing on what you deliver vs when or where you do it. Which, for the most part, is great news for new parents who need more flexibility than most.

3. Explore the advantages and disadvantages of working from home

Again, depending on the nature of your role and your organization, working from home may be a serious option that you are entertaining. The many upsides of working from home a large majority of us have directly experienced in recent years; however, do carefully again consider your motivations. If it's to help you manage drop-off and pick-up then all to the good. If, however you're thinking you'll be able to work from home with your child there, I'd encourage you to reconsider. Even if you have help at home in the form of a nanny or family member, it can be incredibly distracting hearing your child. One to consider. Also, in the new world of hybrid working there is a risk parents work from home more than non-parents and are therefore less visible and may not only miss out on the collaboration/social side of being with others but also on career opportunities (more on this in Chapter 9). For now, though, consider how it would work in practice, and if there are any reasonable concerns this could raise so you're ready for any pushback.

4. Consider a change in start/finish time

A simple change in start or finish time can make a huge difference to some people. It may be, for example, you want to do drop-offs and your partner pick-ups (or vice versa). Shifting your hours slightly can enable you to do this and take the pressure off. As many parents will tell you from bitter experience, there is nothing worse than being under pressure to handover your child whilst having one eye on the watch and the first meeting/appointment you have to get to. It definitely does not make for a good experience for anyone! And it will hang over you all day if you rush away. Feeding our enemy, guilt, something big and chunky to get its teeth sunk into, at your expense.

You can imagine the similar scenario at pick-up for anyone making a mental note to negotiate for picks-up vs drop-offs with their partner. Seeing your child is the last one at pick-up is guaranteed to pull at your heart strings and add to that the irritated look of your childcare provider if you're late, and it's not the first time. The other thing on timing to seriously consider, if it's an option for you, is working much more flexible hours altogether. Many parents – particularly solo parents or those with school-age children – work very happily with breaks in their day. For example, they work 9–3 then again 8–10 to make up the time. This can also be really helpful if you hold a global role with time differences to factor in.

5. Do some homework

Are there other parents at your organization that have 'been there and done that' that you can talk to? How did they make it work? Any lessons learned or advice they can share? Not only will it help you to feel less alone, but it may be they can give you ideas of new arrangements to consider or even provide a case study to share with your manager to back up your recommendation.

6. Get informed

Double check your company policy. It may have changed since you went on leave. It may be that, like many organizations, they are more open to flexible arrangements than they were historically. The key thing here is to avoid making any assumptions and get an understanding of what might be possible/what framework you are operating within.

When you're ready to talk about it

Okay, so now you have a clearer idea of what you want, it's time to think about how you have the best possible conversation on this.

1. Consider the reaction

You know what you want, and you may have a gut feeling about how that will be received. Or you may be feeling very unsure. Take a moment to reflect on that.

Firstly, what is it based on? It might be you had a conversation with your manager before you went on leave. It may be the stories you've heard about the experiences of others. The point is, whether you're expecting a good or bad reaction (or are feeling very unsure) may be based on assumptions vs fact. And even if it is more factual, something may have changed. That's not meant to panic you, it's meant to make sure you're not surprised by the reaction you get, or unfairly assume the worst, which could in turn impact your behaviour.

Secondly, if you think there may be objections raised to what you're suggesting, consider how you could address these. What you could do to allay any concerns. If you think there's a strong chance of this you may even want to pre-empt this by raising it and talking through your thoughts on how to overcome any potential issues. Also be aware, whoever you need to gain agreement from may also be reacting based on assumptions. Try to be open-minded about this and give them time to digest what you're suggesting. Don't expect an immediate answer. Getting the right one sometimes takes time.

2. Talk about it first

Having diligently done all your research on what models your colleagues have adopted and what your company policies are, don't be tempted to jump in and submit a form without discussing it. Why not? Firstly, you effectively set off a ticking clock. In the UK, anyone working for an employer for more than 26 weeks has a legal entitlement to request flexible working (and soon, if not already by the time you read this, it will be a day one right).[2] That obviously doesn't mean it will be granted, but it means the employer has to consider it and as such there are timeframes associated with it. We're back to avoiding adding pressure, which is not something anyone wants. But secondly, and I think far more importantly, you want to make this a discussion. If you don't, you risk missing the chance to find a solution which is better for everyone. And of course, you also risk a flat no, instead of a tweak that turns a no into a yes. Think about the formal process as paperwork to file once you've reached an agreement rather than how you reach that agreement.

3. Present several options and a recommendation

Treat this like you would any other work challenge. Present the issue (for example, 'I would like to return on a four-day week because I want to spend more time with my new child'), then present some potential solutions (which days you're thinking about and why, how this might affect your work and the team, how you think you'll overcome any challenges you can foresee) and then your recommendation (which you think is the best option and why). And then listen. Really listen. Try to understand any concerns they have. See it from their point of view. Make it clear you're open to discussing other options. Work it through together as a problem to be solved rather than a you vs them. They may have thought of challenges – or better solutions – that you have not. I can't stress too much how important this is in finding an arrangement that will not only be something you're happy with but will be successful. And if you can't get there in your first meeting, suggest a follow up to give you both time to digest and come up with other ideas.

4. Consider doing a trial

If you're finding it difficult to reach an arrangement that you're both 100% happy with, consider doing a trial – and suggesting this as a way forward. This can be particularly helpful if your manager has concerns about how you'll get your job done with whatever it is you're proposing and you're convinced you can make it work. It gives you a chance to prove it can work without them fully committing to anything on a permanent basis.

If you go this route, I'd highly recommend making sure you have long enough to give it a fair shot (say three months), getting a date in the diary to review how it's going and, perhaps most importantly, agreeing up front how you're going to judge if it's been a success – or not. It can also be really helpful to check in regularly during the trial period to see how it's going – for them and for you. You may feel everything's working really well and be unaware of concerns they may have. The sooner you know about them, the sooner you have an opportunity to address them. And before you get to the end of the trial period.

I did something similar myself at Sky. As I mentioned earlier, when I first returned from maternity leave, I moved from five days to four days. Fast forward a few years, my daughter had started school and I found, as so many people do, that getting childcare to fit around a school day, which is shorter than a working day, is challenging. There are options, of course, but I decided at that point I wanted to be around more. On a very personal level it was at that point becoming clearer to us that we may not be lucky enough to have a second child, which was also influencing our thinking. Not missing out on the one we had therefore became a bigger priority than it might otherwise have been. The nature of my role at that time was that I was working on multiple projects for various internal clients. It therefore seemed logical to me that I could reduce my hours and just reduce the number of projects in line with that. The key to making it work was being available on a regular basis.

Following my own advice above, I approached my manager and took them through my thinking and suggested a model where I worked three days over four. I knew three full days would prove challenging and I was fortunate that I only lived 20 minutes away from our office, so doing two full days and two half days was totally feasible. They accepted it in principle but we both wanted to make sure it would work in practice so agreed a three-month trial period. Success for us was simply I was (a) happy it was working for me, and (b) delivering what I needed to be with no negative knock-on impacts at work (which, to be fair, was also part of my own measure of being happy it was working for me!).

It only took a couple of weeks to realize it wasn't working. At least, not quite. We'd agreed a pattern whereby I worked a half-day Monday, all Tuesday, all Thursday and a half-day again on a Friday, with Wednesdays off (as before). The problem was it felt stop start. I didn't know if I was coming or going. I don't think we even had a formal conversation. It was just one of those where we looked at each other and said, 'Something needs to change doesn't it?'

We switched so that I instead worked a full day Monday and a half-day Tuesday, meaning I extended my mid-week break to a day and a half. It sounds like such a small change, but it was transformational. I was in full-on work mode Mondays and Tuesday mornings then switched into parent mode before back into work mode Thursday mornings. I felt fully there for each role rather than having a toe in each. We didn't make it to the end of the three-month trial before making it permanent.

And in case anyone is wondering about how you can make that work at a senior level, it may help to hear that about a year in I had a chat with a member of our Executive management team. I mentioned my working pattern and they were open-mouthed. They had no idea I even worked part time, let alone three days. As you can tell, I am a big believer in output being everything.

Of course, this is just one example, in one country, one industry and one job type. There must be an infinite number of potential solutions to working flexibly, and as you can see even from my examples, what works really well for a couple of years may need to be changed as your family grows. The key message here is work through it together to give yourself the best chance of finding something that works – and works well.

Exercise 5.1: What's your ideal working pattern?

Before we move on, take a moment to note how you're feeling about your working pattern going forwards at this point.

What's your objective? What are you hoping to achieve and why? What are the must-haves vs the nice-to-haves?

What potential solutions are you considering proposing at this point? Would it be a formal or informal arrangement? Is a trial worth suggesting?

What do you think the reaction might be? What's driving this? How could you address any concerns?

What else do you need to find out to help you? Who do you need to speak to?

Keep revisiting this – as you've probably guessed, how you feel about this is likely to change over time. And the more time you can give yourself before you need to discuss it the better. But remember it is a conversation, so don't get yourself entrenched in a position either. Look at the conversation as the first step towards agreeing a new way of working.

Once you've agreed a new working arrangement

Big relief. You've got a new working arrangement you're hopefully feeling good about. Now you can file that paperwork, complete the forms on whatever system and start looking ahead and preparing for your return. A couple of last things to consider here.

Make sure you understand the implications

Firstly, just triple check you understand what this will mean in terms of your benefits – I'm thinking specifically about any childcare schemes and holidays here. Public holidays, in particular, if you're changing to a part-time arrangement and making sure you understand how these will be treated. Most organizations pro-rata holidays when you go part time to make sure it's fair (to you and your colleagues) if you don't normally work on the days public holidays tend to fall but it's worth being clear so there are no surprises.

Think about who needs to know

Secondly, and the bigger one – think about how you will communicate your new arrangement. Start by having a think and discussing with your manager who else needs to know about your new arrangement and work out how and when to tell them. This is where that list of stakeholders we talked about in Chapter 3 can be really helpful if you made one. If you didn't, don't panic – just make one now. It's likely to include members of your immediate team, those in other teams around your organization you work closely with, any external clients or suppliers, and senior stakeholders. Some you may not need to formally tell at all, hence the surprise of the leader I mentioned earlier when they found out I was part time years later. Make the list and then work through it, decide if you feel it would be helpful to tell them and, if so, when would be a good time. Whether that should be before you return or something you're happy to cover the first time you see them when you get back. And think about the order you tell people too (for example, all key internal people before any externals).

The nature of your role, your organization's approach to flexible working and of course the changes you are making will likely determine whether each is a straightforward conversation (or even email) or one that needs to be handled more carefully. For example, you might expect a client who is used to you being available what feels like 24/7 to have a first reaction based around 'What will that mean for me?'. You may anticipate a similar reaction from team members who instinctively fear they will be picking up the slack when you're not there. In the same way you approached the conversation with your manager, try and see this from their point of view. What reasonable concerns might they have? How could you address these? You then know how to present the news to them and hopefully minimize the chance of a bad reaction.

Without wishing to sound negative, that doesn't mean you can entirely prevent a bad reaction. But, if you put thought into what challenges it may throw up, encourage them to share their concerns and listen and work it through together, there is a lot less risk of this. A lot of the time it comes down to communication and assumptions being made.

I want to share a story here that is rooted around home schooling during the pandemic but hopefully illustrates the point I'm making. I was talking to a very old friend of mine, who is in a senior role at a major consultancy firm. They do not have any children. They were sharing their frustrations that parents in their team were emailing at all hours, and they felt that because they didn't have children they were expected to respond immediately. That they didn't have the 'excuse' of looking after children in the evening and whilst in lockdown they clearly couldn't say they were out!

I then shared what my typical day was looking like at that point. Up at 5 am, straight to work until 8 am when my daughter got up and the builders arrived – yes, we were mad enough to start a major renovation project on our house in 2020! – then I had zero mental bandwidth to deal with anything but home school and the daily barrage of questions and issues thrown up by the project. After lunch, as many people did, we got our fresh air, and then at 4 pm when the builders left and my daughter had finished schoolwork and could be otherwise entertained for a couple of hours, I'd start work again before stopping for dinner, then re-starting about 8/8.30 pm.

My friend was speechless. I didn't have to explain the reason I sent emails late at night was because that was one of the only times I could, and I in no way expected people to respond then. They got it.

OK, so this is a bit of an extreme example and for anyone thinking I'm a head case, I assure you this was short term (and I know of many worse stories from parents during lockdown). And there are, of course, also alternatives like the 'schedule send' to delay your emails (which can be brilliant but also has its downsides if someone replies before your carefully crafted message arrives!), but the point I'm trying to illustrate is just how easy it is to jump to conclusions. To assume that because you leave on time/early to get to pick-up that you're not working as hard as your child-free colleagues.

It is my sincere hope – and happily what I'm hearing from organizations all the time – that this is changing. The pandemic and the associated overnight switch to remote working for many of us has left us with that positive legacy. But it isn't universal, and you may still come up against these kinds of fears and concerns. So best to be prepared for them.

Step 4: Creating a return plan

You have agreed a date you'll return; what else is there? For some people, it is as simple as that. However, there are some options to consider and decisions to make – for example:

- **KIT days:** I've mentioned KIT days before. If these are an option, now is the time to decide (if you haven't already) if you want to make use of these.
- **Straight back vs ramp up:** it's also the time to decide whether you want to just jump straight back in or ramp up

your return more gradually using either KIT days, accrued annual leave or a combination of the two.

- **Accrued annual leave:** and to think about using some of that accrued leave to start getting paid again before you actually return.

If you decide some of the above sound like something you might want to do, you obviously need to create a plan for this and agree it with your manager. Let's go through each of them in turn.

KIT days

As noted in Part 1 (see Chapter 3) these are designed to help you stay in touch with the organization while you're on leave by working up to 10 days. They are totally optional – both the employee and employer need to agree to them. However, in my experience, the majority of UK employers are now very supportive of their use as they recognize the value in helping with the handover and making your transition back that much smoother. And those who use them find them really valuable for the same reasons – and, of course, the added bonus of some additional pay. There is an equivalent provision for those on Shared Parental Leave (SPL) known as SPLIT days; the only difference is you can take more of them – 20 days – and, believe it or not, these are in addition to KIT days.[3]

In practice, though, for most people 10 days is more than enough and while occasionally I come across someone who has spread them throughout their leave, the majority use them towards the end of their leave as a way to start reconnecting. To dip your toes back in and make sure you don't miss out on key events like team offsites, big client/project meetings or training days that are happening in the weeks before your official return.

KIT days are also a great way to help you and your child get used to what it will be like when you go back to work. I've found a lot of employers are relaxed about the hours you do, allowing you to claim for them when coming in for one or two meetings, e.g. to meet your manager to talk through a return plan and so on. So, if this is the first time you have left your child with someone else it might be a way to do this for only half a day initially, which is easier on both of you. Food for thought and again totally something you and your manager need to agree between you.

Straight back in vs ramp up

Starting with one or two days a week and building up to your full working pattern, whatever that looks like, can make your transition back feel less abrupt and is definitely worth considering. Your instinctive reaction may be to wonder what that would mean in practice. If it would be possible with your role. If it's something your organization would agree to. At the very least, it's something I always encourage people to take a moment to think about it. To work out if it's right for you. If it could be helpful – or not. And if you'd like to explore it further, have the conversation and find out if it would work in practice for you and your team.

Why would you do this? It's quite a big change to go from full-time caring straight back into a full-time job (or even a part-time job). Both for you and your child. Phasing this change in over a few weeks can make it feel much less daunting all round. It's a great way to get used to leaving your child in the care of another (for them and for you) and help you get back up to speed without feeling overwhelmed. You could even look at your team diary and make sure the days you're in are the key ones for training, workshops etc.

Sounds good, but how can you achieve it? There are two main ways you can 'ramp up' on your return. The first involves KIT days. Most UK employees are aware of them but don't always think of them as a way to ramp up. In my experience, fewer are aware of the second way — the fact that they have accrued annual leave while being away — and how to potentially use both alongside each other.

This last point is key. KIT days can only be used while you're on parental leave. Annual leave can only be taken when you're back. So, you have to use these in the right order.

Timeline shows when annual leave and KIT or SPLIT days can be used

Maternity/Adoption/ SPL Start Date		Return Date	
Annual Leave ⇓	**KIT/SPLIT Days**	⇓	**Annual Leave**

Note: KIT/SPLIT Days can only be used while on Maternity/Adoption or SPL and accrued annual leave can only be used before or after

Let's start with KIT days. As mentioned above, you can request up to 10 KIT days (and if relevant 20 SPLIT days) before your official return date, and there is no reason why you can't plan these to gradually increase the number of hours/days you work each week. Which is exactly what I did.

Before I went on leave, we had openly discussed using the 10 KIT Day allowance to help me get back up to speed ahead of my actual return date. I don't think I used any of them in the first six months I was on leave but in the last few months I found them incredibly useful. There were a couple of big team days I was able to join and then in the last few weeks before I returned, I used them to 'ramp up' slowly, working initially one day a week then two and so on to the extent that when my actual return date came it didn't feel like such a big deal. I was already involved in new projects, had met new team members and, importantly, had also had an opportunity to start getting more comfortable with leaving my daughter and getting used to my childcare before it was my new day-to-day reality.

What I wasn't really up to speed with was annual leave. I remember being aware that I had accrued annual leave while being away (and delighted, if I'm honest, when I found out!) but it never occurred to either my manager or me to use any of it before I returned. When you add what you've accrued while being on leave together with your regular entitlement for the rest of your holiday year it can be a lot. I had something like 35 days I had to use in six months. That's seven weeks of leave (well, nearly nine on a four-day week). Lovely as it sounds, initially it can be a problem. Fitting it all in and still being able to do your job. And it can also feel like a waste. If only you could make better use of it… which is exactly my point.

A great way to use some of it is to help you ramp up. The big upside being you start getting paid for your full working pattern but work fewer days initially by having one, two or three days a week off on leave. From an employer's point of view this may have the added benefit of you returning earlier than you might otherwise have done.

It's worth flagging the point made in Chapter 3, that a small, albeit increasing number of companies are offering employees the opportunity to return on a part-time basis for full-time pay for the first X months (typically six months). It may be you are one of those lucky enough to benefit from this, so you have that to factor into your plans as well!

Accrued annual leave

While you're on parental leave, you may continue to accrue both statutory and contractual annual leave in the same way as if you had been at work. This depends on the organization you work for and where you are in the world – and for some countries it is only for a set period.

In Germany, for example, it applies to the mandatory maternity leave six weeks before and eight weeks after your baby is due and any month you take parental leave but work at least one day of that month, but not any full months of parental leave you take.[4]

In the USA, there is no provision for accruing annual leave while on parental leave. This is, however, at the discretion of employers, so it's worth checking your organization's policy. Multinational organizations in particular may offer this (along with other benefits) to be in line with their policies in the other countries in which they operate. You may also find it's possible to use paid time off (PTO) as part of your parental leave.

In the UK, you accrue annual leave for the entire duration of your parental leave. That means both the paid annual leave your contract with your employer gives you and potentially public holidays as well (unless your employer includes bank holidays as part of your statutory annual leave – if you think this might be you, bear this in mind when reading the example below and seek specialist advice).[5] But, yes – for most people that means paid leave AND any bank holidays while you are on leave.

As in my example, this can mean you return to work with a huge number of days to take off and many employers want you to take that before the end of your holiday year or within X months if they allow you to carry it over. Clearly, aside from your own employers' policies a lot will depend on how long you have been away and how this lands against your holiday year.

How much annual leave will you accrue?

Let's take a look at this using an easy example:

- You take the full 12 months' leave, starting 1 July (let's call it Year 1)
- You are returning 1 July the following year (Year 2)
- You get 25 days paid holiday and your employers holiday year is a standard January to December

This would mean you would accrue any outstanding leave from Year 1. In this example that would be a maximum of 25 days if you had taken no holiday at all before going on leave, plus the bank holidays from 1 July to 31 December, typically August and Christmas x2, giving you a total of 28 days.

In Year 2 you would accrue annual leave for the first six months of the year (12.5 days) together with the bank holidays – normally New Year, Easter x2, Spring x2 – giving you a further 17.5 days. That means in theory you could return with 45.5 days' annual leave owing to you. That's a lot in anyone's book. Just over nine weeks of leave to use within six months. And that's if you return on a full-time basis.

I should note that, in reality, not only are you highly unlikely to take no leave before your maternity, but a lot of organizations also have a policy requiring you to take at least some of this before you go, which will reduce this. They can also insist you use some on your return. But this is very much organization dependent, and many will be happy to find a solution which works for you both. And of course, it gets more complex still if your organization offers unlimited annual leave.

So, where do you start? Once you know your return date, you can do the maths – and get help from either your manager or your people team to confirm – so you know exactly what your entitlement will be. Then consider if that's reasonable for you to use in the timeframe. Or, if it would actually be more helpful to you to use some of that leave before you officially return.

As well as making sure you don't have an excessive amount of annual leave before you start your parental leave (see Chapter 3) this also presents an opportunity for your return plan. You could also choose to make your *actual* return date (when you literally start working again) different to your *official* return date (when your parental leave is over, and you are day 1 back in the organization and being paid again as normal) by using some of your annual leave. In other words, agree a return date, but instead of physically returning on day 1, use a week or two's leave (or whatever you agree) to delay that but start getting paid again (assuming you have reached the end of any enhanced pay by this point).

The obvious challenge here some of you may already have spotted is what happens if you want to ramp up your return with KIT days and also effectively extend your parental leave using your accrued leave? There's no easy way around this. You just have to work through what makes most sense for you within the limitations of how you can use each.

How much annual leave will you accrue while on leave?

Your Accrued Leave is the sum of A + B + C where:
A = how much annual leave you have left during the holiday year when you start your leave
B = how many public holidays there will be while you are on leave
C = how much annual leave you would have been due the year you return from maternity leave on your return date

Leave Start Date   **Return Date**
1 July Y1   **1 July Y2**

Jan	Mar	May	July	Sept	Nov	Jan	Mar	May	July	Sept	Nov
		YEAR 1							YEAR 2		

Working   Parental Leave   Working

A: Annual leave left*

B: Number of public holidays

C: Annual leave due

On your return you will have the total of A+B+C (your accrued leave)
AND
whatever you will be due before the end of the holiday year

* This is simply your annual entitlement less days already taken

How much annual leave will you accrue while on leave?

Example scenario

In the written example:
A = 25 days
B = 8
C = 12.5 days

Total = 45.5 days

Alternative examples

Scenario 2 - same holiday entitlement but you've taken 15 days already and only take 6 months maternity so return Jan 1st Y2**:
A = 10 (25-15)
B = 3
C = 0

Total = 13 (**in practice Jan 2nd in the UK as this is a public holiday but this would be paid leave as a returned employee).

Scenario 3 - same holiday entitlement, you've taken 15 days already and take a full 12 months maternity leave from the start of November Y1 so return 1 Nov Y2:
A = 10 (25-15)
B = 8
C = 21 (rounded up)

Total = 39

Note: with a Jan to Dec holiday year, returning towards the end of it as in this example means you potentially have more leave than you can use in a short amount of time (2 months in this example) – specially when you factor in the additional amount due before the end of the year (the extra 4 days) taking you to 43 days…

Creating your own return to work plan

This can very quickly get quite complicated, and I suspect a few people have had to read even my 'easy example' more than once to get your head around it. I double-checked this a few times while writing! And as you may have noted there is an almost infinite number of ways you could use these tools to stagger or adapt your return, so, to try and help bring it to life, here are some of the more common scenarios, along with a representation in table form.

- **Parent 1** – wants to use some KIT days to reconnect and ramp up their return slowly ahead of their return date but not use any of their accrued annual leave
- **Parent 2** – wants to use both KIT days and annual leave to ramp up their return gradually, which in effect means they aren't full time until some weeks after their official return date
- **Parent 3** – wants to tag some of their accrued leave onto the end of their parental leave so they start to get paid before they go back
- **Parent 4** – wants to use their annual leave to work part time for the first X weeks/months back

Sample return to work plans

Return to work date

	Week -4	Week -3	Week -2	Week -1	Week 1	Week 2	Week 3	Week 4
Parent 1	1 KIT day	2 KIT days	3 KIT days	4 KIT days				
Parent 2	2 KIT day	2 KIT days	3 KIT days	3 KIT days	2 days leave	2 days leave	1 days leave	1 days leave
Parent 3					5 days leave	5 days leave		
Parent 4					1 days leave	1 days leave	1 days leave	1 days leave

Note: for simplicity, all of these examples assume someone is returning 5 days/week but they could easily be adapted to shorter weeks.

Your return to work plan

Here's a blank template for you to work out what different options might look like and create your own return to work plan.

Return to work date

	Week -4	Week -3	Week -2	Week -1	Week 1	Week 2	Week 3	Week 4
Option 1:								
Option 2:								
Option 3:								
Option 4:								

Key takeaways from this chapter

- Remember there are timelines to work to – in the UK you need to agree your return date eight weeks before
- Start the conversations earlier if you want to make any changes to your role or working pattern – give yourself and your manager enough time to talk through the options and agree a plan together
- If you want to change your working pattern, consider if it needs to be a formal or informal arrangement and dig deep to find a solution that's right for you AND the organization
- When you're ready to, present several options and a recommendation, talk it through and work out a solution together with your manager
- If you do make a formal change, use the formal process as the paperwork once you've agreed your new working arrangement
- When creating your return plan, find out what options you have available to you in terms of KIT/SPLIT days and accrued annual leave
- Consider ramping up and how you could achieve this remembering KIT/SPLIT days can only be used while you're on parental leave and annual leave can only be take when you're back

If you're supporting your partner/someone close to you

Help them work through what it is they ideally want, and what this might mean for them/your family/their team. Is there anything going on at home that is influencing their thinking? Are there any other options you could consider?

If you're supporting someone in your team

Be open to reconnecting, and if they're asking for a different working arrangement, try and get clarity on what's driving their request and, rather than immediately think about the challenges, ask yourself – what would it take to make it work? What alternative solutions can you see? Would a trial be helpful? What is going on that they may not be aware of that could influence their thinking? Also – and this is a really important one – be careful not to make assumptions about their aspirations just because of their personal circumstances or because they want to work in a different way. Listen to them and if you're not sure, ask. Do they just want to get used to their new normal or are they interested in a new role – now?

Chapter 6

Planning for a smooth return to the organization

Now you've got your return date sorted, and you have an idea of what you want that return to look like, what else can you do to prepare yourself for actually going back? In this chapter, we'll focus on Step 5 (from the steps outlined at the beginning of Chapter 5): Prepare for your return – the practical actions you can take to give yourself the best chance of minimizing any bumps along the way both work wise and at home.

Again, we'll use a checklist format to make it easier to jump over any parts you already feel confident about and also refer back later to those you feel need more thought.

Preparing for your return – at work

Time to get into the detail. What you can do to make those first few days and weeks back smoother for you and your team.

☐ Create a plan for your first day/week/month back

You've been thinking about it for so long, but you might not have thought more practically about day one. Week one. What do they look like? Try to imagine you're back in your workplace. Will you literally just step back into your role from the first minute? Clearly, the answer to this question depends a great deal on your role, but for the majority the answer is no. There's a lot to catch up on.

I have people tell me, often with some frustration, that they were treated like they had never been away and others that they were treated like someone totally new (particularly by those who have joined in their absence). In reality, neither is accurate. It takes a bit of time to get back up to speed, but nothing like as much as someone completely new to the organization. And, of course, others aren't always sure how to behave around you. This is why helping shape those first days and weeks back can be so helpful. Not just to you, but to others as well.

Some new team joiners didn't realize I'd worked here for years!

(Recently returned parent)

So have a think about what would be really useful to you. What might be really useful to your manager. Your wider team. The key clients or internal stakeholders you deal with regularly. And perhaps, more importantly, what is realistic. There is no point in creating a plan that makes you feel like you're under huge amounts of pressure, getting to the end of the first day, week or month and feeling like a failure as you haven't completed an enormous to-do list! That's not what I mean. You want to think about what would help you feel good when you look back on those first few weeks back. What's going to be important in helping you feel that way. Your list will be totally personal but may include, for example:

- Catching up with all your team
- Meeting any key new faces
- Getting up to speed with the latest projects

- Understanding team priorities and getting clear on how you fit in
- Reconnecting with clients and/or suppliers and understanding their current focus and any challenges
- Learning how to use any new systems/processes

And make sure the timeframes work for you as well. The most important people, like your manager and any direct reports will probably be day one, your priorities might be week one, then meetings with all clients by the end of the first month... you get the idea.

☐ Make sure your tech is set up

This is perfect for a KIT Day, if you're using them. Alternatively, allow some time for this in your first few days back. Again, it depends on your role but for most of us now there are a lot of systems/logins we need to access on a daily basis, and passwords expire, systems are updated... you can already imagine, I'm sure. The last thing you want is to be struggling to access something you need for your first meeting. If you made a list pre-leave, it's time to dust it off and use it to help you get started. Don't be afraid to ask team members and/or your manager for help here too. If this is nagging at the back of your mind, you may even want to flag it and arrange some time with your Technology team or a tech-savvy colleague for when you come in.

☐ Find out about major events

Another useful question to ask is what major events are coming up in the weeks before and after your return date. There may be team offsites or training days, big team socials like a Christmas lunch/party, or a big client review day. These will, of course, vary depending on your employer and role, but whatever they are, make sure you know when they're coming up. This can be very helpful in planning any KIT days or accrued annual leave if you're using them, and also for planning ahead with childcare, if needed.

A lot of first-time parents in particular find this one of the harder things to get used to. Deciding whether to go along to team socials or out-of-hours networking events might have been straightforward before. You only had your own social life to juggle. Now you have the limits of childcare to factor in and maybe your partner's diary too. You can see where I'm going with this. It gets a lot more complicated very quickly. It's normally doable; it just takes planning and therefore a bit more advance warning than you may be used to. Spontaneous outings are a thing of the past – well, for a period anyway.

If your colleagues don't have young children themselves, it will take them time as well to adjust to you needing a little more notice if they want you to join them. And it may be helpful to consider lunches instead of evening events, if this is easier for you. Bear in mind you may also be helping others – not just other parents but, for example, team members who don't drink or those who have caring responsibilities for older members of their family and therefore cannot make evenings. Some people find it easier to ask if they know that accommodating their needs also helps to make team events more inclusive generally.

☐ Arrange a meeting with your manager on Day 1

Having a meeting with your manager in the diary for your first day back can be really helpful for both of you, so if they haven't already arranged this it's well worth reaching out and suggesting it. They are your first port of call for a lot of the subjects we've already covered, and many more besides. What you cover is likely to depend on whether it is literally your first day back or you have been ramping up slowly with KIT days etc., but the sorts of things you can consider for the agenda are:

- **Organization priorities** – getting an update on changes in the organization priorities while you've been on leave, current focus, and even what's gone well, what hasn't
- **Team priorities/your priorities** – what this means for your team and your role, where you'll need to focus your efforts/what's going to be important in the next year
- **Team changes** – who's joined the team, who's left
- **Client/stakeholders/suppliers** – any changes in the key people you work with
- **Immediate priorities/expectations** – what they want from you in your first weeks back
- **Any specific support you need** – anything you think you'll need to help you or questions you have, for example on breastfeeding facilities, or how you'll manage getting out on time on the day your regular team meeting takes place and tends to run over... you get the idea.

I realize this is a big list and I'm not suggesting you have to tackle it all in one go! The intention is to help you start thinking about what's going to be most helpful for you personally on that first day back vs what you don't need to cover or what can wait a little. The questions burning in your mind that you want to ask, that are going to put you at ease and help your day to day go smoothly. Think of this as a chance to set the tone for your return. To have a discussion that will set you both off on the right foot and help keep those all-important lines of communication open.

☐ Start thinking about your boundaries

This is a topic we'll cover in more depth in Part 3, but I want to touch on it now as it can be really useful to start thinking about this before you're back in the thick of it. Before you're feeling under pressure. What do I mean? Firstly, to be aware of your limitations – when you are going to have to arrive or leave at specific times. When you won't be able to get in early or leave a little bit late. And secondly, to start thinking of the boundaries you want to create, such as making being home for bath time a priority or making sure you manage it at least X times a week and so on.

If you're sharing parental leave

A note here if you and your partner are sharing parental leave, and one of you is returning while the other is taking on being the primary carer for a while. Again, more on this in Part 3, but bear in mind what works for you in those first few months when you have the security of your partner looking after your child may be different from when your partner has also returned to work. It's easy to slip into a working routine that works short term but might not be what you want/need in the long term – and changing it after just a few months may be harder all round than implementing your long-term plan from the start.

If you're adopting

And a note for those adopting. Think about what you're prepared to share about your child's history before they joined your family – and what you're not. One adopted father explained, 'I've spent a lot of time fending off questions about their earlier life', and how 'triggering' this can be. Inevitably, there is a story with any adoption, and it's likely you'll feel that's very personal to you and your family. Maybe, as this father said, 'it's not my story to tell'. Or perhaps you need to keep their identity private for their safety. People often ask without thinking, mostly from a good place, that you've done an amazing thing, but it's definitely worth being ready for how you answer that. And equally aware of this if someone you know is adopting.

I've spent a lot of time fending off questions about their earlier life.

(Adoptive dad)

☐ Consider carefully what informal flexibility you will need

In the previous chapter, we looked at what formal flexibility you would need. Now it's time to look at what *informal* flexibility you might need. The ad hoc type. Everyone needs flexibility. Yes, *everyone*. Not just parents.

I remember chatting with a C-Suite Executive about this (and for those not familiar with this term, C-Suite is basically an organization's senior executives, those whose titles often begin with a 'C', like the Chief Executive Officer and Chief Financial Officer). I asked if they worked flexibly and they said 'No', without hesitation. I was aware they had children, so I asked if they went to any of their sports days, school concerts etc. 'Yes, absolutely', they responded. My next question was if they took annual leave to attend them. Their face started to register what I was getting at, and they said 'No', they didn't… they worked flexibly already and hadn't even realized it. Many people don't, which is why people often only associate flexibility with parents, or worse, mothers.

The latter point was reinforced for me by a father in a same-sex relationship who is the primary carer. Flexibility is still so often only associated with working mothers. Working fathers (and non-parents, I might add) are all too often forgotten. For a father who is the primary carer this can be particularly frustrating. He told me he'd ended up saying 'think of me as the mum' to try and get the message across. It makes it simple but it's a shame he felt he had to do that for people to understand.

This is changing, of course, and the pandemic has done a lot to accelerate that change, but it's still an important distinction to draw. And it's important to recognize you are going to need it more than most. Even if you hold a C-Suite role.

OK, so what kind of flexibility are you going to need on an ad hoc basis? That's the million-dollar question! There are some predictable events, like doctor's appointments, sports days, school concerts and so on, but you will most often need extra flexibility when you least expect it. And as per Murphy's Law, these are likely to be at the worst possible times.

I had my own version of this back when my daughter was very small. We found ourselves unexpectedly with no childcare, indefinitely, and it was a week when I had a major presentation to our Executive team. Typical, right? If I'm honest, it was a bit of a rabbit in headlights moment. Time to take a deep breath. I remember a slightly tense initial conversation with my husband as we tried to divide up the week depending on who really needed to be in the office which days and therefore who could be at home, and quickly realized we needed more than that.

The conversation that really helped me was with my manager. I feel it's only fair to say they are one of the best I have ever had, and it wasn't just because they were really inspiring on the work front. It was also because in these crucial moments (and there were others), they listened calmly and helped me work through them. They pointed out that the only day I really needed to be in the office was the day of the presentation. The rest we could work around. And this was before the days that video calls were second nature. They were also aware of my childcare arrangements and that my parents helped us. And that was the start of the plan.

My mum came up to be there the day of the presentation. Cue a huge sigh of relief and moving from panic into action mode. And if you're wondering how we managed the rest of it, we used an agency to get an emergency nanny to come to our house. I realize this won't be an option for everyone, but an increasing number of organizations now subsidize this kind of back-up support. Add to this, the increase in hybrid working means juggling working remotely while you get through this kind of challenge is a more realistic option for many today.

The main point here is we found a way to bridge the gap while we worked on a longer-term solution, which we managed to sort within a couple of weeks. Drama over. And for what it's worth, we ended up with a much better arrangement as well. In addition to a valuable lesson. You get through this stuff!

There is always a way…

(Author)

What specifically did I learn though?

- **It can be helpful to talk about your childcare arrangements at work** – particularly with your manager. The more they know about your situation, the more they will be able to empathize and help you when you need it.
- **Break it down** – when you're in a tight spot, which can be by its very nature emotional, try and step back and look at it objectively. Much like the conversation around your working

arrangement. Try and get clear on the key challenge, and what options you have to solve it.

- **Expect challenges and know you will manage them** – you will inevitably face some challenges when your work life and your home life collide. There is, of course, only so much you can do to prepare for them, but being ready to accept they will happen is a good start.

And this is where we start to segue neatly into the next section.

Preparing for your return – at home

There are actions you can take at home to help ease your transition back to work.

☐ Create a back-up plan

This is for when things go wrong. Whether that's a childcare breakdown (as in the previous example) or your child being unwell, it can be really helpful to have a go-to list or plan. To have discussed with your partner in advance who's on point which days – I know many couples who go through their diaries every weekend and agree exactly that. A list of people you can call on if needed to help can also be really useful, particularly if you're a single parent. And if you're feeling like it's all on you because you don't have family or support locally, don't be too disheartened at this stage; you'll very quickly find people – whether it's a friend with small children, or a nursery nurse looking for extra hours and so on – who may be able to help you.

☐ Think through and explore all the childcare options

Having reliable childcare in place that you feel really confident about makes a huge difference to your mindset. Imagine for a moment you're feeling unsure about the nursery, you had some niggling doubts and you ignored them. Now you're back at work. Guess what's front of mind? The new project you've been asked to get up to speed on or whether you've made the wrong choice and if your child is going to be okay at the end of the day. I'm not saying you can magically block out thoughts or concerns about your child with perfect childcare – if only! – but hopefully you can see the point I'm trying to make. The happier you feel with your childcare choices, the better the chance you are giving yourself to focus most of your attention on your work role.

Finding the right childcare is a big challenge. Sometimes it feels difficult to know where to start. There are many options, nurseries, childminders, nannies, family or friends. See Chapter 3 for the overview of the common options. It is not my intention, or expertise, to offer advice on these but it is definitely worth considering all the different options available to you. Obviously, what you can afford will be a big factor. As well as the location and implications for any commute you have.

More than that, it may be that a combination of different options is a good solution for your family. For example, you might have a nursery place a few days a week and then a grandparent looking after your baby one or two days a week.

The other really important thing to remember is that nothing is forever. It's very easy in the early stages of parenthood to feel like the solution you have is a long-term commitment. Not that you want to be changing your arrangements on a regular basis, but you will probably find you naturally outgrow what you have in place from time to time. Your nursery staff may change. Your own job might change, impacting where you need your childcare to be, or when. So, whilst it's absolutely worth making every effort to find a solution you feel really comfortable with, if it doesn't work out it's not a disaster; you can find another solution.

☐ Consider a settling in period with your childcare

Whether you choose to ramp up your return or just jump straight back in, it's worth considering a settling in period with your chosen childcare, to help both you and your child adjust. Most nurseries will suggest this anyway and being able to leave them the first time and be available to pick them up as needed is a lot less stressful than attempting to combine this with your first day back! It also means you can consider doing just a few hours and building it up. Effectively ramping up their time away from you so that by the time you go back it's become normal. And of course, there's the added benefit that it can buy you a few child-free hours to do some of the other prep we've talked about – or just have some no doubt much needed me time!

☐ Have a conversation at home

It's very easy to slip into roles, whereby the partner at home takes on all the family admin in addition to being the primary carer – and it stays that way when they return to work. In fact, the moment you return to work can in some ways feel like it's a bigger shock for the partner who has worked throughout (perhaps a brief period of paternity leave aside) than your child arriving in the world in the first place.

It's therefore a key moment to have a conversation – or several – about how you will manage logistics and rebalance the load at home going forward. Everything from pick-ups and drop-offs, to who cooks, who does the weekly shop, household bills and so on. I've included a couple of templates you may find useful to get you started, which can be adapted to suit your own needs.

Weekday Childcare Plan

	Mon	Tues	Weds	Thurs	Fri
Get ready					
Drop-off					
On point for any issues					
Pick-up					
Bath/bedtime					
Prep for next day					

Note: assumes regular Mon–Fri working pattern but please adapt as needed.

Family Admin Review

What	Who's currently responsible (you/your partner/shared)	Talk about changing?
Cleaning the house		
Changing beds		
Washing/ironing		
Grocery shopping		
Cooking		
Bins		
Gardening		
Cars		
Shopping for kids		
Birthday presents/ parties		
Family social plans		

Holiday planning		
Medical appointments		
Finance planning		
House repairs		
Pet care		
Childcare providers		
Bills		

These templates are a great way to see at a glance who is doing what, when, and review it together. You might find it helpful to break it down further and even consider the amount of effort involved in each, but you get the idea…

And it's important to note that this is not just about admin and dishing out tasks. It's a key opportunity to think about and agree how your family operates going forwards. Do you want one of you to be the primary carer? Or split things more evenly? And this isn't black and white – think about what's going to work for you. Once you're both back at work, your new routine will quickly become habit, a habit that in many cases doesn't change for years. So, this is a golden time to think about what you want as a family, and how you make that happen. I don't want to stereotype, but I'm thinking of dads in particular here – if you want to look back and have been there, think about what that means day to day, what you're there for (e.g. bath time X days a week) and how you can make that happen.

If you're sharing parental leave and your partner is taking over the caring role, then it's more a conversation about switching roles at this point and, if you feel up to it, even reviewing what's worked well and what hasn't so far and making some changes.

Finances permitting, it's also the time to consider hiring in outside help (if you haven't already) – especially if you're a single parent. In fact, this is where I think some single parents lead the way. They are quicker to realize you can't always do it all, and as one solo parent said to me:

Recognize what only you can do, and what you can outsource.

(Experienced solo parent)

☐ Check your 'work wardrobe'

I say this with a little bit of nervousness, if I'm honest. I don't in any way want to body shame anyone. Far from it. And besides, this applies as much to new dads as new mums. A friend who is a new dad and was about to return to work after taking surrogacy leave said it really struck a chord with him, too, 'not being able to do the same fitness routine… not much sleeping etc. took its toll'. He went on to say:

A refresh felt like a nice thing to do for yourself…
and helps give a little boost to confidence.

(Recently returned parent)

And that's the main aim – ensuring you feel the most confident you can. If you've had a baby your body has been through a lot and may not have totally gone back to how it was before. And even if it has, or you're not the birth mother but have been on parental leave for months, it can be helpful to make sure you have clothes that make you feel good about yourself in those early days back. In a recent session, someone told me how grateful they were for this suggestion. That it hadn't even crossed their mind and they knew it would have been a last-minute panic the week before returning, so they were hugely grateful for the heads up!

You might also find your feet have grown in size if you have been pregnant. Yes, really! I had noticed my own feet seemed to be a bit larger but not significant enough to need to change shoe size, and I hadn't connected it with pregnancy until a friend told me 'my feet went up half a size'. If you google it, it really is a thing!

My feet went up half a size.

(Mum, post-baby)

☐ Consider any upcoming personal appointments

Here I'm talking about the routine doctor and dentist appointments, eye tests etc. Not because you shouldn't fit these in around your working pattern but because anything you can do to reduce pressure in those first few weeks back will pay back dividends for your state of mind. Give yourself the chance to focus all of your attention on making the transition – for you and your child – as smooth as possible, without anything else to factor in.

☐ Consider seeking and accepting help from friends/family

There's a lot to think about and do before your return to work. And that's not easy when you're looking after a little one. So, if you have offers of help, now's a good time to consider accepting them. Buy yourself some time to get ready, physically and mentally. Maybe even carve out some all-important 'me time'. It's in everyone's interests for you to put yourself in the best possible place to tackle this. And for what it's worth, I'd argue the same is true earlier in your leave. An hour here or there is such a gift.

An old friend of my husband, who I didn't know that well at that point, offered to give me a couple of hours to myself when my daughter was small and I was on leave. I was a little hesitant if I'm honest, but it did me the world of good. I have always remembered that kindness and it helped me to realize that accepting help can be a very positive thing all round.

Exercise 6.1: What's front of mind as you plan your return?

Having read through these, what's front of mind for you now? You might find it useful to fill out this template with actions to take.

Where	What	Who	When
Is this a challenge, home or work?	Is it you need to do?	Do you need to talk to/help from?	Is a good time to aim to do this/is there a deadline?

Key takeaways from this chapter

- Think in advance about what a good first day/week/month back would look like so you set yourself realistic goals and can get yourself back on track when needed
- Remember the little things that can make a difference and help you avoid slip ups, like sorting your tech out and being aware of major events
- Ensure you carve out time to meet with your manager early on to give you both an opportunity to talk about what's changed and agree your priorities
- Start thinking about what your boundaries might be, what's really important to you, what you'll be able to control and what you won't
- Don't forget to consider the impact of returning to work on your home life and what might need to change for you as a family going forwards

If you're supporting your partner/someone close to you

Help them think through what's realistic in those early days and weeks and not put too much pressure on themselves. Consider and discuss carefully what their return will mean for your (or their) family. Use it as an opportunity and start as you mean to go on. What do you want your family life to look like with you both working? How much do you want to be involved? What changes might this mean for your own ways of working?

If you're supporting someone in your team

Give some thought ahead of their return to what you can do to help them settle back in as quickly as possible. What's changed since they've been away? Have you got a one-to-one in the diary and are you clear on their early priorities/what you're keen to discuss? Have you asked them about any needs on their return such as breastfeeding facilities? Can you arrange a team lunch and/or a buddy for them (ideally someone who has also recently returned)?

Reflections on Part 2

As we come to the end of Part 2, it's worth taking a moment to reflect on the challenges as your thoughts turn to returning to work. How are you feeling about your return? What are you really clear about and what do you need to do more thinking on/need some help with?

Exercise 6.2: What are your takeaways from Part 2?

What are your key outstanding concerns?	Who could help? What actions could you take?

Part 3

Returning to work

Chapter 7

Recognizing the challenges of coming back

You're finally back. After all that planning, the conversations, and maybe some KIT days thrown in, the day is here. And whether you were able to ramp up slowly or simply returned, the date still feels like a big one. It's a moment to be marked when you officially move from being a full-time parent to being a working parent. You did it!

Let's be clear, not everyone manages this. Yes, some by choice, but some who would like to don't make it back, so do take a moment to recognize this success – for you and your employer. That doesn't mean the end of challenges, though. In some ways, this is just the beginning. And that's not meant to frighten or overwhelm you. It's just reality. Being a working parent brings many challenges. Challenges you will overcome, I hasten to add. And for many people, the initial period following their parental leave is the toughest, so that's where we're going to focus now.

In this chapter, we take a look at the challenges you're likely to face as you begin to re-integrate back into your workplace and adjust to your new dual roles of parent and employee.

What's on your mind as you make the transition back?

Let's start at a high level again with the common themes…

Practical

Your day to day is likely looking very different already than before you had a child. Whatever childcare route you have taken, you now have a whole layer of responsibilities before your official working day even begins and then again when it finishes. Sometimes in between as well. I took to calling my job my 'day job' because it felt like my real job now was being a parent. And it was – and is – an all-consuming job at that.

Emotional

Although the day to day can leave you exhausted, it is perhaps the emotional that is the most draining. It's a big adjustment going from being with your child almost 24/7 to away from them for a significant chunk of the week and leaving them in the care of others. It's hard to let go and very easy to worry. Combine this with the challenge of trying to find time for everything and guilt really starts to rear its ugly head too.

Cultural

Finally, not only might you be feeling differently about your career, so might others – including those who are in a position to influence your future career progression. Then there's the home front to think about too. It can take some time for everyone to adjust.

Exercise 7.1: How are you feeling about your return to work?

As at the start of the previous two parts of the book, let's take a moment to recognise how you're feeling about your return today, right now, and make some notes below. As ever, there is no right or wrong answer here. And, perhaps more than ever, how you feel (or felt) on your first day back might be very different to the end of the first week back or six weeks in.

Try not to refer back to your notes/answers in Chapters 1 and 4 at this point. Again, your thoughts are likely to have evolved still further.

For now, I want you to ask yourself the following questions and right down the first thoughts that come to mind. Be really honest with yourself. No one else is going to read this list unless you choose to share it with them or get them to help you with it. And no thought is irrelevant. If it's on your mind, write it down. And again, look at this as a living list that grows with you. Revisit it as often as you like as you progress through the book.

What are you feeling really good about? What's working well?

What are you finding are the biggest challenges? Or what will they be?

What do you think is most likely to have an impact on your overcoming these?

Once you've done this, take a moment to process what's on your mind.

The top 10 most common concerns at this point

Time to take a closer look at the common concerns at this point.

1. Adapting to someone else looking after your child

This is a big one for a lot of people. It may be the first time you've entrusted the care of your child to someone else. And whilst in the early days it can be a bit of a shock for many to go from being an individual to having a small person who in some ways feels like they are permanently attached to you, it's amazing how quickly that becomes the norm. How quickly it starts to feel comforting, even. And so, to then take them away again and be wandering around the world again on your own (at least some of the time!) can feel very strange. Not all bad, I might add, it can be liberating too, but with a dose of 'mental load'.

But that's only the tip of the iceberg. Leaving your child with one of your parents, for example, is a big enough step for some. To leave them with a relative stranger, albeit a professional, can frankly be very unnerving. Even frightening. What if something happens to them while you're not there?

Then there's the extended family support. Whilst for many it's not only something they're incredibly grateful for – both on an emotional level because it feels better leaving your child with family and less pressurized, and from a financial point of view – it doesn't come without its own challenges. It's harder to set boundaries, particularly around how you want your child brought up, for example, what they're allowed to do, what they eat etc. And it's harder to talk through any issues. It's far from impossible, though, and in fact many families both rely on and really value this support and what it brings to their family relationships.

And if you're sharing parental leave you have a switch in roles to navigate, which can be hard for both of you.

2. Exhaustion

I don't think anyone would argue that the first few months after you have a baby are totally exhausting. Sleep deprivation is a special form of torture. Everything can become very blurry, very quickly. But if you're one of the lucky ones, and your baby takes to sleeping through relatively quickly, you may be in a good place by the time you return to work. Adding work into the mix can throw that right out of the window. And if you're not one of those lucky ones it can be downright rough.

You may recall I mentioned earlier how I began referring to my job as my 'day job'. It felt like my job was a bit of time away from my real job of being a parent, which was otherwise 24/7. And if that sounds strange, remember we pay people to look after our children while we work. For them it is their job. But one they only do for the X hours a day you are at work (or travelling to and from).

They are tired at the end of the day. Just like you will be. You may have forgotten how much work takes out of you. Adjusting to that on top of parenting takes a bit of time. You may find yourself functioning pretty well while you're at work, then collapsing afterwards and struggling to do everything at home. Or you may find you're so tired you're struggling to stay awake in meetings. It happens.

And if you're adopting and thinking 'what about me?', there are additional elements to consider. The adoption process itself is exhausting, particularly emotionally. And that's before your child officially becomes part of your family. Integrating your new family can also be tough. If you don't have a young baby, you are also likely dealing with a child who has experienced trauma. I take my hat off to anyone who has or is doing this. Be kind to yourself. Particularly in the early stages.

3. Re-integrating into the team

Some people find it really easy to slot back into their role and their team, but for a lot of people they find they're feeling really anxious about this. A new manager or a lot of new team members can increase the chances of feeling like that. So can being the only parent of a new baby. It's a stage filled with unique challenges which can be isolating.

When I re-joined my team, I was the only one with a baby at that point. I was lucky; everyone from my manager to colleagues and beyond were really supportive. But they weren't going through it at that point. It made me feel different. And despite being an extrovert, it made it hard to share some of the challenges I was facing. I felt I was bothering them. And as I said, I consider myself one of the lucky ones. Some people feel they are being treated differently. For example, not being given the same type of work as it's assumed they won't be up for it. Or not being invited to team get-togethers as it's assumed they won't be able to make it. Notice I've used the word 'assumed' there twice. That's because it's often assumptions that are at the root of some of these issues.

4. Practicalities

What seem like sensible security policies can actually cause issues for those on or returning from parental leave. My email was cut off a month into my maternity leave and I remember having a small panic and wondering if my P45 was in the post (for those outside the UK this is basically a piece of paper your employer gives you when you leave a job – or you've been fired!). I've heard many other people talk about being locked out of their email/IT systems and even buildings. Their security passes no longer working. These are relatively simple fixes but, in the moment, they can be not only frustrating but also make people feel really excluded. Not considered. And it's also a little embarrassing. The same is true for things like breastfeeding facilities. If there isn't anywhere you know of it can be embarrassing to have to ask or, worse, make do with the inappropriate (using a pump in a loo is neither fun nor hygienic).

5. Juggling everything

This is probably one of the most talked about topics associated with working parents and the reason I have mentioned it in all three parts of the book. How do we do it all? How indeed! Life can feel like a constant juggle and perhaps no more so than when you first return to work. You're being pulled in a million different directions. Your to-do list seems endless. Sound familiar?

In the spirit of being upfront, I'm not suggesting this is a challenge that will go away. But it will get easier. Or, at least, easier to deal with because in time you'll have gained some invaluable experience of managing this ever-present challenge of the working parent. And as with many things, how you approach it can be a huge difference. So, our aim here is to help you get there sooner.

> *I found myself juggling work and managing expectations internally and with clients.*
>
> (Recently returned parent)

6. Managing the clashes

I'm calling this out separately as, in my experience, this is a big issue in its own right. When people talk about juggling, they are usually talking about getting all their work done in the hours they have, and/ or being there for their child when they feel they should be. Clashes are something else. They happen when your work life and home life have a specific conflict. When you can't be in two places at once. When a meeting overruns and you're supposed to be on your way to pick up your child. When your child throws a major tantrum in the morning, and you end up being late to work. When you're asked to attend a meeting outside of your normal working hours. And as your child gets bigger, there will be school plays, sports days and so on to somehow fit in. Sometimes you can plan around these, particularly when you have notice, but sometimes you can't. Schools the world over, it seems, are famous for last-minute changes: 'Your child is in tomorrow morning's assembly' is a particular favourite of mine. 'Please, mama, why can't you come?' Tough to deal with.

7. Guilt – at work and at home

This leads us nicely onto our old foe, guilt. I don't think I've ever spoken to a working parent who hasn't felt guilt at some point, and for many of us it makes a regular appearance. 'I'm not doing a good enough job at work/home' – delete as appropriate. It's so very easy to find you're berating yourself. If one part of your life is going well, you'll often find the other part is suffering – or at least that's how you perceive it. And perception is a big part of the battle here. As one recently returned parent said to me: 'I'm feeling unreliable', as they explained how they were feeling about sometimes being late in or having to leave early, and then went on to acknowledge, 'it's not always, or even usually, how others perceive me'. We'll unpick this a bit more in the next chapter.

> *How do I get over the guilt that I feel about not being at home/*
> *school for everything?*

(Returning mum with an older child as well)

8. Wellbeing

Looking after yourself often drops right to the bottom of the list when you're a new parent, and this is perhaps particularly true when you first return to work. It might feel that there is too much else occupying both your mind and your time to even think about this, let alone do something about it. Take heart; you are not alone. However much it might feel like a luxury you just can't afford right now, remember that looking after yourself is probably the most important thing you can do. And if that still feels selfish, look at it another way. If you're not in a good place, do you think you're going to be the best parent you can be? The best employee? Team member? Partner? Friend? You see where I'm going with this. And if you think I'm having a laugh suggesting it's something you can carve out time for, it might not be as hard as you think (even as a single parent). For now, just let this sink in and remember the first thoughts that are popping into your mind as you read this, the things you want to do for yourself that you have perhaps let slide.

9. The impact on your career progression

Assumptions also play a key role in career progression. They can lead to being overlooked for promotion opportunities, or at least feeling like you are being overlooked or passed over. Then there's the impact of your leave on the promotion that was talked about before. I have heard many people express concerns that they'll have to 'prove myself all over again' or that they feel their leave has set them back. Of course, this should not be the case at all, and I can happily also share I know of people being promoted while they are on leave. So, this is by no means an inevitable issue, but it is very much a concern shared by many.

10. Making it work when you have a global role

I'm calling this out even though it might seem quite specific, just because more and more people have roles which involve them dealing with clients or colleagues who are working in different time zones (me included). You might even have a manager in a different time zone. This presents some very specific challenges, even without children. Throw a young child into the mix and it becomes that much harder. You can't do a morning nursery run in London when you're supposed to be on a 7 am with Sydney or equally make a 7 pm call with the west coast of the USA whilst putting your baby to bed. It causes a lot of anxiety for new parents in these kinds of roles. How will you be able to do the role you did before and be there for your child?

Revisit your list

As we wrap up the chapter, time to revisit your list from the start. Anything else to add? Or that you're even starting to feel a little better about or have a better understanding of why you're feeling that way?

Key takeaways from this chapter

- Be honest with yourself about what's on your mind as you return to work, what you're loving, and what you're finding hard
- Remember you are not alone, the challenges are not unique to you and there is a way to overcome them
- Always bear in mind it's a period of huge change, both at work and at home which is exhausting in itself without adding sleep deprivation to the mix!

If you're supporting your partner/someone close to you

Try and help them identify their biggest challenges and, perhaps more importantly, what is driving them. Is there anything you can already see that might make a difference? Maybe something you (or they) could change today to help – practically or emotionally?

If you're supporting someone in your team

Be aware the first few weeks in particular can be really tough for a new parent. They will often try to put a 'brave face' on but may be really struggling underneath. What do you think are likely to be the key challenges for them? What could you do to help lighten the load for them? But don't forget to not make assumptions – keep talking to them. Find out how they are and what you can do to help.

Chapter 8

Working out how to overcome challenges and who can help

We have yet another new set of challenges. Some are short term, some longer term. Some you can tackle alone but a lot of them will require support or input from others. Where do you start? In this chapter we will start by looking at what you can do in your first few weeks and months back and then a bit longer term. At your 'new normal'. And I feel the need to defend this phrase at this point as one I was using pre-Covid! Essentially, though, we're looking at what might help once you're past the initial return and coming up for air. I refer to it as the 'meerkat moment' – when you metaphorically sit up and realize this is your life now and maybe start to look at things differently. We'll also be dusting off the list of people around you who might be able to help from Chapter 2.

Your first few weeks/months back

This can be one of those times where you're in survival mode. Trying to re-adjust to work alongside childcare and juggling the extra curveballs life is throwing at you along the way. You rarely get a moment to yourself, and it may feel like you don't have time to think, let alone take on board any ideas, but there are some simple things you can do that might help ease the pressure.

☐ Give yourself time to adjust

Don't be too hard on yourself. I can't emphasize this enough. It takes time to adjust and, to use what I know is a slightly overused term right now, it is very much a journey. One you find yourself constantly learning on. In fact, it is probably the ultimate learn-on-the-job role you will ever have. And to quote Rachel Vecht, Founder and Director, Educating Matters, who I count as a friend as well as being fortunate to work with: 'In many ways, it's the hardest job you'll ever have, with the least amount of training!'

As your child develops and grows, so does your role as their parent. I often feel that just as soon as I've got the hang of whatever situation, something else happens to make me feel I'm playing catch up again! And this has inevitable knock-on impacts on your day job. Be kind to yourself, particularly in those early days and weeks when it can feel you're fighting to keep your head above water. Seek out others in the same boat. Others who are facing the same challenges. It really does help to know you are not alone.

☐ Review and extend your plan for your first weeks/ months back

This of course assumes you did this when reading Chapter 6. Don't worry if you didn't or haven't yet! Now is a great time to start. And if you have done it, take time to review it, update it and extend it to cover your first three months back.

Imagine someone asked you after three months how your return had gone and your answer was along the lines of 'couldn't have gone better'. What would have happened for you to feel like that? What would good look like for you? What would you feel both proud of in terms of what you have achieved and would make you feel good? It can be helpful to then work that back and, if it helps motivate you, create small milestones.

It might be as simple as that by three months you feel you're back up to speed and have reconnected with everyone you wanted to, you've ironed out any practicalities like breastfeeding at work and logins, and you feel ownership over your key responsibilities and part of the team again. Or there might be some very specific goals you want to set yourself. It might be around a promotion you have been working towards or delivering a particular project. It's a very personal review with no judgement from anyone apart from yourself. My only caution would be to be mindful of doing too little or too much. Neither will be helpful to you. So, think about what you feel is reasonable. And, of course, as things change in those three months do allow yourself to adjust this accordingly. It's not meant to be a straitjacket, more a life raft with a GPS to help you feel you're in a good place at the end of those first three months.

I've included a template below to help you get started.

Exercise 8.1: Planning your first three months back

What might be on your three-month plan? This is likely to include practical actions (like reconnecting with keep people) and more difficult to measure things (like feeling part of the team). For the practical actions list specifics (which people?) and for the more difficult try and unpick what it would take (e.g. for feeling part of the team, it might mean contributing at team meetings, feeling on top of your work and feeling like someone people look to for advice and so on).

Aim	What does that mean to you?	When
E.g. reconnecting	E.g. who to meet up with	Is this something you'd like to achieve by week one, month one, month three?

☐ Be aware of any relevant rights

Just as before you went on leave, make sure you find out what might be relevant for you on your return. I'm thinking in particular here about parental leave and emergency leave. And the parental leave I'm talking about here is the more specific leave available in many countries in addition to the initial period of maternity/paternity/adoption/shared parental leave. As mentioned in the Explainer 'Global variations in support for new parents' in Chapter 3, this can quickly get confusing as in some countries it is typically taken as an extension of that initial period of leave (in Germany, for example) whereas in others it's used separately – the UK being a prime example.

I used parental leave when my daughter started school to help cover the long school summer holidays. And yes, you may be thinking that's a long way off, but you may have more immediate needs and, in my experience, not that many people are aware of this option. See the glossary for more details of the current provision. Many countries offer it as available in chunks after you have returned to work. Something to be aware of.

Similarly, emergency leave, which is also available in many countries, enables you to take time off, as the name suggests, in emergencies. It's designed to help you deal with an immediate situation – when you need to drop everything and go. Parent or not. Again, I found myself in need of this. More on this to follow.

The point is to find out what options you might have so that as and when you should need them, you are aware and you can use them to help make life that little bit easier when it's at its most challenging.

☐ Make the most of any 'quiet' time

Sometimes, granted not always, the first few weeks back can be a bit of a golden time. You might find you don't have your usual full workload as yet. Seize this opportunity with both hands! Work your way through your list of people to reconnect with. Enjoy it. You've got lots to talk about, and people will be pleased to see you. It's a chance to start to rebuild your network, which will not only make doing your job easier but also help you feel part of the team again much more quickly. And don't feel you're slacking off if you're someone that really enjoys this. It's an incredibly important step and one your manager is likely to encourage. Equally, it may be a good time to freshen up your skills, particularly if you have a more technical role or one that uses particular systems. Have a think about what's most helpful and go for it.

☐ Be open to talking and reviewing your new ways of working

Work closely with your manager and key colleagues to make sure your working pattern is working for you and the organization. Even if you haven't changed your working pattern per se, you are likely to be needing more informal flexibility. Is this causing any issues? Are you struggling to get away when you need to? Is there anything they can do to help? Making sure you keep an open line of communication on this from the start will make it much easier to address issues as they arise and prevent them from becoming bigger issues.

One situation I've noticed coming up increasingly is new parents struggling with work outside of normal hours. This could be a site meeting on a construction site or a call with someone in a different time zone. The challenge is essentially the same. How can you make this work around childcare? One strategy I've found helpful links closely to the next point on boundaries. Instead of letting work time bleed into your home time, consider taking control and agreeing (formally or informally) to work different hours on particular days. Start and finish late on Mondays or Thursdays, for example, so you have one evening a week where you can make those calls/attend that meeting without feeling compromised. And most importantly, take the time back at another point – maybe start late that day and have a bit of me time before you start work. Or drop your child late to childcare that day. It might not be quite how you'd envisaged when you returned, but it doesn't mean you can't tweak your arrangements, if that works for all.

Equally, the more comfortable you can get being open about your home life and the challenges the better. I think a real upside of the pandemic was how much our home lives became very visible. We all became more than just the role we do in our day-to-day jobs. It's a great leveller and relationship builder. Don't be afraid to answer honestly when a colleague who can see you're struggling asks how you are. To share what you're going through. They may surprise you in being able to relate, maybe having been there and done that. Even having some tips. Or at the very least, being a sympathetic ear. And by sharing when you're struggling but coping can also be helpful in the times when you really can't do it alone and need help from colleagues.

☐ Be honest about your boundaries

Be honest with yourself as much as anyone else. Are you comfortable being contacted out of hours/on your day off? Has this changed since before you had a child? If you're working to a new pattern, do you want to reflect this on your email signature or out of office?

There is no right or wrong here but it's helpful to recognize how you feel so you effectively have guidelines you work to. Guidelines that you are comfortable with and will in turn give you confidence to make those decisions when you need to.

Personally, I chose not to put an out of office on when I worked part time. I didn't want people to be constantly getting this and I made the choice to check my email on my days off – but with specific limits. I would check my email first thing, and then once later in the day. If something was super urgent and a simple reply or forwarding to a colleague would help, I would respond, and if it wasn't, I would leave them. This typically took only 10 minutes a day in total, and for me it helped my day job because I had answers for things I needed when I was back in the office. My being out hadn't slowed things up. It gave me the peace of mind to be in the moment with my daughter the rest of the time and it really worked for me. But I have colleagues I hugely respect who take the opposite view and put an out of office on and totally switch off on their days off. Both are equally valid approaches.

A bit of a side note here: I have also noticed an increasing number of people adding 'I am sending this email at a time that suits me' to their email footers to take the pressure off recipients from feeling the need to respond straight away. One to consider if you are picking up work again later in the day. Or as we talked about earlier, use the schedule/delay send function. Play around and work out what's best for you and your role.

☐ Consider building in transition time

One of the most common daily pressures I hear from parents is the stress from either being late to work because of problems at drop-off or a tight commute going wrong or running late for pick-up because a meeting has run over/they had to finish something at work. If you're finding this is something that is causing you a regular headache, try building in some transition time.

If you have the ability to block out your diary for the first and last 30 minutes of your day, it can transform your experience. I started doing it when my daughter was little, and I haven't looked back. I've actually found I've come to cherish these blocks of time in my day. If things have gone well, I have bought myself a clear 30 minutes to get my head around the day ahead, remind myself of my priorities and deal with anything urgent before my day kicks off properly. And similarly, in the evening I have time to reflect on the day, and, crucially for me, write a to-do list for my next working day. This helps me mentally clear my mind of work so that when I'm with my daughter I've not got something small niggling at the back of my mind.

Of course, it doesn't always work but if you can make it your norm then the odd days when things go belly up won't feel quite as bad.

☐ Agree your priorities

It's a good idea to make sure that when you meet with your manager you regularly talk through your priorities so you're both really clear. This is especially important if you're working more flexibly or to a different working pattern than before you went on leave. And vital, I would suggest, if you're trialling a new working arrangement. The last thing anyone wants is to find themselves with very different views on how things are going.

You might also want to discuss who else would benefit from knowing what your priorities are and how you'll communicate them. I'm thinking in particular here of your wider team and key stakeholders/clients. This is obviously generally good practice, but it can be a particularly useful time to do this exercise because people naturally make assumptions if you don't. And if your role has changed since before you went on leave, either in what you're responsible for, or when, or if you've changed your working pattern, then this is a particularly risky time for this to happen.

Imagine for a moment you're coming back to the same role but on fewer days than before. Be careful not to fall into the trap of trying to do the same volume of work in fewer hours. Hopefully this is one you have already covered off in your conversations when agreeing your new arrangement. But that's in theory. Now it's real. And you may be your own worst enemy at this point. Remember how you decided you could make this work. What your focus would be. What you agreed you would be responsible for and, perhaps, what you are not responsible for any more. Remind yourself and your manager of this regularly. And by this I don't mean bluntly, 'That's not my job!'.

A good way to approach this is to talk through priorities. Suggest a list of what you plan to focus on in the time you have and sense check this with them. Is that in line with their thinking? That way, if there's something that's at risk of being missed, they (and you) have an opportunity to address it and agree how you'll manage that. Whether that be dropping something else instead, getting extra help from someone else in the team and so on. And if your stomach is sinking when I mention someone else in the team and you're thinking they'll resent what you might see as covering you, try to reframe this. It may be a development opportunity for someone more junior. Or simply a reshuffle of responsibilities across the team.

☐ Discuss your career aspirations

Once you've been back a few weeks, and assuming they haven't already suggested it, get a meeting in the diary with your manager to talk through your career aspirations. As we talked through in Chapter 3 there are very few times when a period of parental leave dovetails nicely into an organization's performance review timetable. And the chances are you will have missed one. That doesn't mean begging for a full appraisal (I have experienced enough as both a manager and individual to know the downsides as well as the up!), but sharing your thinking, and how this has or hasn't changed since you went on leave can be really helpful. Not just for you in gaining feedback and food for thought, but for your manager in being really clear on what you want so that next time an appropriate opportunity arises they think of you.

And to be clear, I'm not just talking about the next promotion here; it can also be helpful in terms of how you develop your skills and experience in your current role – what projects you get assigned, what other responsibilities you'd be interested in taking on, the types of roles you'd like to find out more about, who you could shadow and so on.

☐ Develop lines you're comfortable with when you face the inevitable clashes

And yes, they are inevitable. Unless you have a stay-at-home partner or live-in help there will be clashes. And even then, they may not be able to do everything, particularly if you have more than one child. You may not want them to.

Some of the clashes you'll have some advance warning of, like how you keep your promise to your child to go to sports day when that important meeting has just gone in the diary the same day. Others will hijack your day, like the dreaded call from your childcare provider that your little one is running a temperature and you need to drop everything now to pick them up.

So, knowing you will face them, how do you manage those clashes? And here I'm not so much talking about arranging cover or rescheduling meetings, but the arguably harder part – how do you position these? How do you manage how these are perceived? What I'm getting at here is the way you manage the situation, what you say and do can have a big impact on people's views. Now you could argue (and a big part of me hopes you already are as you read) that no one should judge you for being a parent. And you'd be right, but it's not an easy thing to talk about. It can make you feel on the back foot. And worse, the need to apologize. That is exactly the point. There is no need to apologize for being a parent.

Let me bring this to life a little. I needed to set up a meeting with a senior stakeholder. His PA was offering a Friday afternoon. At that point I wasn't working Friday afternoons. I immediately felt uncomfortable. Guilty. Yes, really. I felt bad I wasn't able to say yes. I even started thinking about how I could come in. I had to give myself a bit of a talking to. I realized there were a million reasons I might not be able to make that day and time. I could be on annual leave. I could be at a training session. I could be at another meeting. I didn't need to explain why I couldn't make it. I just needed to go back with alternatives and find another time. Simple as that. The pressure I felt was entirely internal.

Of course, it won't always be that way. Sometimes the pressure will be external. But the old saying that no one can make you feel anything is totally true. You may feel they are judging you – and the sad truth is maybe they are – but only you can control how you feel. And what you do. So, hold your head high. Think before you respond when you're caught in a difficult situation. And focus on what you can do, rather than what you can't.

☐ Expect hiccups with childcare and have a back-up plan

You might be incredibly lucky and have no issues in those first few weeks and months back, and if that's you, be grateful, as you're very much in the minority! The majority of children, particularly those who go into environments with other kids – whether that be a nursery or with a childminder – will be being exposed to a lot more coughs, colds and other bugs than they're used to. As a result, they tend to end up poorly more often. Which causes you a problem as said nursery or childminder will call you and ask you to take them home before they in turn infect other children. If you're really unlucky, it can feel like an almost weekly event. They're just better and then a few days or a week later they come down with something else. It's exhausting all round. Try to get ahead of this as much as you can by having a bit of a plan to deal with it. It might be, for example, a family member who can step in at short notice (typically but not always grandparents). Or it might be that between you and your partner you work out who is on point which days/weeks. Who can work from home if necessary. As we talked about earlier, many people think about this each weekend, so they have a contingency plan for the week ahead.

Worst case, and assuming both that your child is not incredibly unwell (when of course you just need to be with them, and work needs to take a back seat) and you can afford this, you might want to consider an emergency nanny.

And, of course, there is the 'emergency leave' provision I mentioned earlier which is widely available. It's designed for exactly this sort of situation where you have no choice but to temporarily drop work and sort something out – for example, if your child has chickenpox and can't be in a childcare setting. To be clear, it does not allow you to be off for the entire two weeks (or so) that you will have to isolate your child from others, but it does allow you a day or two to make other arrangements. Whether it's paid or not depends on where you live. In the UK, it is at the discretion of your employer, but in my experience most are pretty generous with this as long as it's not a regular event.

I had to use this myself once. I had a call from my mum – who looked after our daughter once a week – to say she'd slipped and taken a fall. She'd managed to get herself and our (at that point) one-year-old daughter home. But now she couldn't get up. Cue drop everything, mad dash home, ambulance, the works. Thankfully, she wasn't seriously hurt, and our daughter slept through the entire episode – I'm still not sure how we got so lucky on that front!

Some other countries have even better provisions – Germany, for example, entitles employees to sick pay to look after their children when they are unwell.[1] Singapore provides up to six days' paid 'childcare leave' per year to use either when your child is unwell, or even for things like their first day at school or when you find yourself without childcare for whatever reason.[2] Spain has recently implemented a directive on work-life balance which included four days of paid leave for 'urgent and unforeseeable family reasons'.[3]

Whatever comes your way, it's helpful to have considered how you might handle it before, what available options you have and, if you can, have a chat with your manager about it, and also your partner/ those you share childcare with.

☐ Be mindful of establishing short-term patterns if you're sharing leave and your partner is taking over

As mentioned briefly in Chapter 6, be aware if you are in the position that you are returning to work and your partner is on SPL and therefore the primary carer in the short term. As the number of parents take up this option (which is a great trend to see) so I hear about this challenge more and more.

On the one hand, it can make for a much less stressful return to work if you're not having to leave your child in formal childcare. On the other hand, it's very easy to slip back into old habits. Working late. Going out for impromptu team get-togethers. Saying yes to early meetings. And that's great and can really help you feel like your old self again. However, it can set you up for a bit of a fall further down the line. When you partner returns to work, you have to review how you share responsibilities and you may find you have to walk back some of your new (or old) habits. I'm not saying absolutely don't do this, I'm just saying be aware if you are so that you are able to manage your own expectations of yourself, and the expectations of those around you. It might even be a helpful way to frame a conversation around informal flexibility that you will need once you're back.

☐ Try not to make snap decisions

If you're finding the first few weeks back overwhelming it can be tempting to literally throw your hands up in the air and quit. Particularly if you were wrestling with whether you wanted to go back in the first place. And especially if you are finding it emotionally very difficult leaving your child. I've seen it happen. Again, this is clearly a very personal decision, and it might be totally the right decision for you. There is no right or wrong here but, if this is you, I would encourage you to take your time. It's a big decision and a difficult one to reverse, easily at least. Try and break down what it is that you're struggling with and, if you feel comfortable, talk it over with your manager or a trusted colleague. At the very least, talk to your partner and friends. There may be a way through it.

If it is the hours/your working arrangement, don't be afraid to raise this, even if you've had a flexibility request denied before. Strictly speaking, in the UK you don't have the right to make a second request for flexibility within the same year. However, in practice, a lot can change in a year. It may be the right thing for both you and the organization and if you don't ask you'll never know. And if it makes the difference to you staying or going, it may (and I feel the need to stress the *may* part) change the view of your employer. Particularly now you've been back a while. They may have ideas on how to make it work so they don't lose you. It's worth exploring so that, if you do end up leaving, at least neither of you will have any regrets and know you did all you could to make it work.

Your new normal

You've made it through the first few months back and may be starting to wonder what life is going to look like going forwards. A lot of people now pause and even step back to review their lives. They have their 'meerkat moment' I mentioned earlier. It's totally normal and it definitely happened to me. In fact, it's what led me to where I am today.

Remember that moment in front of the mirror I talked about right at the beginning? That was my moment of realization, I guess. When it dawned on me, not so subtly, I might add (more like someone slapping me around the face!), that being a working parent wasn't something I was going to nail within a few weeks or months. It was always going to be challenging, and I had to decide how I was going to handle that. What I wanted my life to look like. As you may recall, I threw myself into setting up the parent network, but as well as being on a mission to help others, it was also very much a way of helping me find the connections I needed at that point. Others going through what I was. And it opened up so much learning and support for me.

It might not be as dramatic for you. It may dawn on you more gradually. And I'm not suggesting you immediately go out and set up a parent network (although if that is of interest and you want some pointers, by all means get in touch; I'm always happy to share what I've learned with others trying to do something similar). Either way, for the majority of people there is a transition from the 'in the thick of it' coping phase into some sort of new day to day which brings with it its own challenges and some ways to cope.

☐ Make sure you don't pass on opportunities to learn and develop

As a newly returned parent you are under pressure from all angles. You will likely find yourself constantly looking for ways to make your life easier and to buy yourself that all-important commodity, time. You might be feeling you're learning so much as a parent you don't have the headspace for learning at work as well. Missing out on a day's training or going to an industry conference or networking event can seem an attractive prospect. 'I don't really need it.' 'I went last year, probably not much new to learn.' 'I know everyone, I don't need to network.' Or 'I'm just too tired right now'.

I'm not saying there won't be some of these that aren't a good use of your time; what I am saying is make sure you judge them fairly. Don't sacrifice your own opportunities to grow professionally. Before long you'll find yourself stagnating in your role. Watching others get promoted over you. And then find you're feeling undervalued. And maybe even thinking about leaving.

That's also why I often see the eyes of managers and people teams light up when I mention this. They get the importance, and they get the risk.

☐ Maintain your profile

It can be hard to maintain your profile when you become a working parent. To make sure you and your achievements are seen. It may not even be something to which you gave much thought to before. I have to be honest, it's not something I ever thought about as a standalone thing. I have always wanted to do well and be recognized for that – but I think that's how most people feel. It certainly wasn't a strategy. However, it was something I became more aware of as I became more senior and became a working parent. The usual opportunities can feel more elusive or downright impractical alongside your childcare responsibilities. You can no longer go out for impromptu catch up with your boss/the team when you have a pick-up to get to. Making time for long chats by the coffee machine can feel like a luxury you can't afford. You have too much to get done before you leave. No option to work late any more. Getting the job done and getting home can seem like a big achievement in itself. You get the point.

But if you continually neglect this, your career may suffer. The best assignments may go to colleagues. The promotion opportunities you might not hear about until too late. And I realize it may feel like a step too far, that I'm asking too much, but it's not as hard as you think.

Just by being aware of it is a great first step. Also, think about ways to highlight your achievements that you feel comfortable with. Particularly if, like for so many, you are not someone who is comfortable shouting about themselves – and despite the stereotype it's not just women, and in fact some women are perfectly comfortable with this approach. Think about what works for you. It may be suggesting you share learnings with the team from a recent project. Or praising the work of someone else on the team for their contribution – thinking of a way you can also be helpful may sit more comfortably with you and make it a 'win win'.

☐ Work out new ways to network

This leads us neatly on to networking. It can fall into the same lower priority trap. But this one applies as much to those who don't feel comfortable with traditional ways of networking as new parents who may not only feel that but are also more time poor. Find ways that you are comfortable with and work within the confines of your new role. If you can't make drinks any more, or at least those at short notice, suggest planning them for a week or two in advance so you have time to arrange childcare. And while we're on the subject of drinks, given the concept is itself not very inclusive of those who don't drink, maybe suggest a team lunch instead or some other way for team bonding (volunteer days, offsites…). If it's one-to-one networking you're looking to do, try meeting for a coffee. If it's raising awareness of a piece of work, try pitching it as sharing learnings for the wider team. And if it's industry connections you're looking for, try signing up to small roundtable events where small talk is replaced by Q&A sessions and finding something in common.

☐ Have an ongoing conversation about ways of working

We touched on this earlier but it's an important one, so I wanted to emphasize this still applies longer term. Whether your working arrangements have changed formally or not, juggling work with a new child is challenging and will have an impact on your job. And these challenges will change, so you need to change with them. Keeping an open dialogue with your manager is crucial. You may feel everything is going fine and they may not, or vice versa. Try and make it a regular agenda item in your one-to-ones. If they're any good it will already be on their radar, but it's something that easily slips to the bottom of the list when dealing with the day to day. Make a point of checking in and making sure they are happy with how things are going. It will give you licence to talk to them when you are finding things more challenging and get their help in finding a way through it, instead of muddling through on your own.

☐ Seek out mentors/buddies/champions

As we've covered several times already, finding sources of support is really important. Those who are going through a similar experience are invaluable, but so are those who just get it. Or get you. People who recognize your value. They can do wonders for your confidence. Think back to that list of sources of support we looked at in Chapter 2. Who are your biggest champions? The ones you have supported your career? Make time to nurture those relationships.

☐ Keep an eye on our old foe, guilt

It can feel like an unwelcome presence, constantly lurking and ready to pounce, and it definitely rears its head from time to time, even amongst the most self-confident of working parents (or frankly parents, full stop). The trick is to be aware when it does, and to try to reframe it.

Let's start with being aware. For some that sounds obvious, but it isn't always. It has a way of sneaking up on you sometimes. Try and learn to recognize the signs. Do you get a sinking feeling? Do you get upset? Frustrated? And if you can recognize what's triggering it, even better. Perhaps it's when you are asked to do something for work at a time you're supposed to be not working. Or you promised yourself you'd be there for bath time and have justified one night won't make any difference, they are too small to notice. You get the idea. Try and recognize what happens for you. What makes you feel that way.

Now comes the arguably difficult bit. How do you limit the damage? And not find yourself getting really upset – potentially on a regular basis. A favourite technique someone once suggested to me was to ask myself in those moments 'Where's the evidence?'. Like most good ideas, it's both very simple and very powerful. Take the earlier example – being asked to do something at a time you're not supposed to be working. Critically here it's likely that you used to work at this time, which is how this gets a hold over you. Where's the evidence? Does the person asking know you don't work at that time? Do they need to? Could you easily do this at a time when you are working? Like the example I shared a little earlier...

Or to take another example: feeling guilty, as you're feeling you're doing less than you used to. Perhaps because you have to leave on time for pick-up. Where's the evidence? Just because you leave earlier than you used to, are you still getting your job done? Did you manage to do everything on your list before you had a child? I suspect not! And are there others having to leave on time to do pick-up?

☐ Be aware of your own wellbeing

As we acknowledged earlier, your own wellbeing can often be something that drops to the bottom of the list. Don't underestimate the impact of this. It might be fine short term but if you constantly put yourself last, it will take a toll.

Whilst definitely relevant to all parents, it's perhaps a point that's critical for single parents. As many have shared with me, it's not just the practical side you have to manage alone, which in itself takes a lot of time as well as energy, it's the emotional. 'Not having someone to talk things through with.' Self-care is hugely important. And if as a single parent that to you means connecting with others and you're finding that difficult practically, online support groups can be a real lifeline. Something to consider.

The Wheel of Life

This brings us neatly on to a favourite tool of mine I'd like to share with you. It's a great way to take a personal temperature check. To see how you're doing. What aspects of your life perhaps need a little attention. I have seen it with multiple names, but I know it as the Wheel of Life. I believe it was first used by John Meyer, one of the founders of life coaching, back in the 1960s. The categories can be amended to suit. Here's one that I think is likely to be helpful to most at this point:

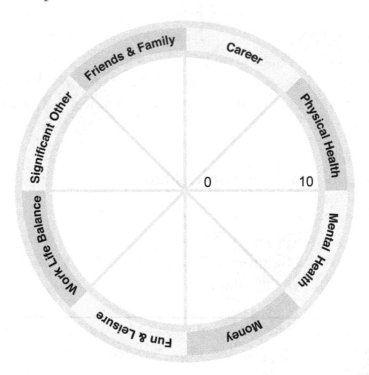

The idea is to look at each area of your life in turn and give it a mark out of 10; 10 is great, really satisfied, 0 is very dissatisfied. It should be a gut reaction, not something you spend a lot of time thinking about. It is likely to help you quickly acknowledge what you probably already knew.

Feelings are like data, use as a temperature check to measure where you are.

(Rachel Vecht, Founder and Director, Educating Matters)

For example, you may be feeling you're not managing to find time for yourself, whether that be for exercise or time with friends, so you score these very low, whereas you feel you're doing well with your work, and everything else is ok, so it might look a bit like this:

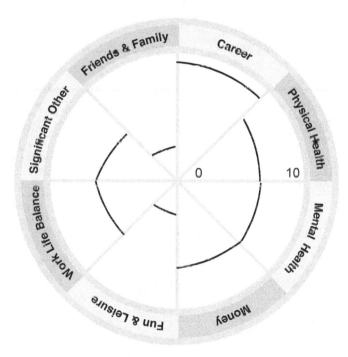

And remember, how you score a category depends on what it means to you. For example, career satisfaction to one person may just mean them feeling they are doing their job, to someone else it would mean not just doing the job but learning and growing ready for the next one.

It is not meant to make you feel bad; it's meant to help focus your mind on what you need to tackle – and that's half the battle – and then think about where you can make changes, and where you can't. For example, it might be that what could make a difference between a low and high score for work-life balance is making it home for bath time each night. Or not feeling quite so rushed in the mornings.

Be aware, it will change over time too, so this a great tool to use on a regular basis. I do.

Key takeaways from this chapter

- It takes time to adjust – be kind to yourself
- Remind yourself of what you thought was reasonable for your first weeks back and think about how that changes as you look ahead to your first three months back
- Keep talking – especially about your ways of working and your boundaries, if they're being stretched or broken, and take actions to change things as needed
- Consider building in transition time to give yourself breathing space and minimize the everyday stresses which tend to accumulate over time
- Get clarity on your priorities and be really clear about your career aspirations to avoid assumptions being made
- Make sure you don't pass on opportunities to build your skills and experience
- Regularly check in on how you're feeling, what's working well and what needs attention, so you have a chance to act before they become a big deal
- Make time for you

If you're supporting your partner/someone close to you

Keep checking in – they may have a great first week back and then it all goes horribly wrong, and they start struggling to cope. Think about what you can do to help. Have you got the balance of responsibilities right at home or could you make changes? Do they have enough support? Remember, it will be a tough time for you too and feeling like you have to hold it together might not be the best long-term solution for your family. Find people you can lean on as well.

If you're supporting someone in your team

Encourage them to use their first few weeks and months back wisely, including focusing in particular on reconnecting. Avoid making assumptions about what they are (and are not) capable of taking on and when. Keep checking in with them and don't assume that, if they were fine in their first week, they will still be in their second month. Monitor their development and workload (especially if they have changed their working pattern). Are they turning down opportunities regularly? Is their workload reasonable? What opportunities can you provide them with to help them settle back in and raise their profile?

Chapter 9

Identifying new skills brought to the workplace

This is one of my favourite parts of the post-leave sessions. And in the sessions I run for managers, come to think of it. As you may have noticed, a large part of the content is focused on the challenges that you will face and how to overcome them. This is the opposite. It's about all the added skills and experience a new parent brings back to the workplace with them when they return. It's not often discussed or recognized, even by parents themselves. And it's *all* positive.

What new or enhanced skills?

What am I talking about? Take a moment to think about it. What has day to day life with a little one taught you? How have you changed how you do things? What are you better at than you used to be? Which might you be using at work without perhaps realizing it? Take notice of the skills you have developed since becoming a parent that are – or will – help you in your day job. Because there will be some. They will be unique to you, but to help you get started, I'll cover some common themes.

Time management

You may find your ability to focus has sharply improved. How you manage your time, now you likely have less of it. Thinking about work specifically, this is more obvious if you are formally working less hours or days than you did before, but even those who have returned on the same basis as they left are likely to find they have less flexibility to work late than they did before.

And if you're thinking, that's okay, I'll pick up later in the evening, yes, that's definitely an option. However, in my experience it's more of an option for those with older children. New parents are generally so exhausted that this will be a tough ask. And, of course, that's assuming they have a job that makes this possible and they don't have their hands full when they get home. Early evening is known as the 'witching hour' for a reason.

Imagine for a moment you've been up the night before, do a full day's work, come home to a little one who is tired, cranky and refusing to go to bed. How much are you feeling like opening the laptop again after dinner? Or is the thought of potentially having to get up again and your sheer exhaustion meaning bed is too much to resist?

Getting it done during your working hours is a much more attractive prospect. And potentially the only realistic one for you. It's also incredibly satisfying.

I remember a particularly pressured day when I was asked to pull together a slide summarizing a project I had just completed for our team meeting the next day. Whilst I was happy to have the opportunity, the first thing that went through my mind was 'When am I going to be able to do this?!' – and yes, I panicked for a moment. I had about 20 minutes until my next meeting and was back-to-back for the rest of the day, then heading home to pick-up and look after my little girl, and I knew doing something that evening was basically out of the question. I quickly accepted my only real option was to do it in that next 20 minutes. Could I really do that?

When am I going to be able to do this?!

(Author)

I sat and thought for a moment about what was being asked of me. Having a battle with my innate perfectionist, I realized essentially it was only one slide of bullet points; I could talk to the rest – that's what the team really wanted to hear anyway. They didn't want a complicated PowerPoint slide. So, I sat there, and thought about it from their point of view, what they'd want to know, and wrote some simple bullet points to that effect. Job done.

Not only did it go really well, it also taught me several valuable lessons. Firstly, not to over-analyse and jump to conclusions about what is needed. Instead, to think about what's really being asked of you and what your audience wants or needs. And secondly, not everything has to be perfect. As I am now very fond of saying:

Done is better than perfect.

(Author)

It's actually a tactic I have used many times since. Particularly when presenting. Deep breath, think about what's needed, what the audience is looking for, keep it simple and allow yourself the freedom to expand on other points as you go. It makes it far more engaging for you and your audience.

But I digress. The key point here is, you will inevitably find yourself in tough spots timewise on a regular basis, but you will also find, I suspect, that you are much more capable of getting more done in that time than you were. You are much more productive. And this will be noticed by others too. As one recently returned parent shared with me, they 'get on and get it done', both at home and at work.

Get on and get it done.

(Recently returned mum)

Perspective

Many people also find their priorities have changed when they have a child. Whilst this may sound obvious, what's less obvious is that one of the by-products is it can often have a positive impact on work – work no longer being the most important thing in your life (if it ever was).

The point is, regardless of your prior relationship with your job, work is a big part of most of our lives and so we understandably feel invested in it. It's in our interests to be. When a child comes along, they demand a lot of our attention. We have to find a way for our dual roles of parent and employee to coexist. I think that our relationship with work often changes as a result.

Many people find work coming lower down in their priorities. That doesn't mean less commitment. But it can help you put the everyday stresses of a job into perspective. To help you feel less emotionally attached to your role. More objective.

It also doesn't mean you're less engaged, and in fact my own personal experience, as well as what I've observed in others, is that many people find they are more engaged with their work after having a child.

This might feel counter-intuitive, and I can hear the objections, but bear with me. It does, of course, depend on the relationship between the employee and employer and a great deal on the way their parental leave has been managed. However, many people find themselves re-evaluating their career choices when they have a child. If they are going to make the trade-off of working vs caring for their child, they want to make sure that time is well spent. I was talking to a parent recently who had returned to work the previous week. They shared that one of their concerns had been 'Would I still enjoy this?'.

I remember going through a similar thought process. I had only just started a new strategy role within Sky, which was an area I had long wanted to get into, when I found out I was pregnant. So, when I returned from maternity the role was still relatively new to me and I still had a lot to learn. My point is, I had every reason to want to go back, more than in my whole career history, but I still questioned if it was the right thing to do.

I had an interest in making it somewhere I wanted to be. To get the most out of my role. I found myself more engaged than I had ever been. But at the same time, I was looking at work with new eyes. I was more careful, more respectful of my own time. How much I could get out of the role being related to what I put in. And it gave me a different perspective. I found I looked at it more objectively. I don't think I needed work to fulfil as many emotional needs as it did before. To be clear, I'm not suggesting everyone will feel that way. Or react that way. But I know I am not alone in looking at my career with fresh eyes and a different perspective, which has helped me.

Empathy

Equally, being a parent, particularly a new parent with so much going on outside of your professional life, tends to remind people the same is true for others. If someone behaves badly towards you, you may find yourself not taking it quite so personally (if this is something you had a tendency to do before, which I think it's fair to say most of us do from time to time at least!). You may find yourself wondering whether they have something else going on, something that's bothering them.

I will own up to having had this experience. More than once. In fact, the two times that spring to mind, the first I was pregnant (before anyone at work knew) and the second a working parent. On both occasions I was blamed – and very publicly – by someone senior for something that had nothing to do with me. On both occasions I ended up in tears in the bathroom. So far, the same. The difference was, the first time, I was cut up about for it ages. And yes, whilst the pregnancy hormones probably exacerbated it, I definitely spent more time thinking about it.

The second time, whilst still very upsetting in the moment, I did immediately start wondering what had driven the behaviour. If there was something else going on in that person's life that had made them behave inappropriately. I didn't blame myself nearly as much – well, as long as you don't count not being stronger in the moment and standing up for myself more... but standing up to those more senior to you, publicly, is another topic altogether. Hopefully you see the point.

This is a very useful skill. Some people are naturally better at this than others but somehow becoming a parent often enhances this even in those of us who are not so naturally gifted.

Management of difficult stakeholders

This one is a bit tongue in cheek, but as most parents will tell you, if you can deal with a toddler in full meltdown, that colleague/manager/big boss throwing their metaphorical toys out of the pram will seem a bit less daunting and something you are more likely to take in your stride!

What about you?

What new skills do you think you have developed, or existing skills have you enhanced since becoming a parent? Take a moment to think about it and use the next exercise to jot down your thoughts.

Exercise 9.1: What skills have you brought back to your workplace after becoming a parent?

Reflect on what's changed for you. Which of the points above resonate with you? Where are you today vs when you first found out you were going to become a parent? I suspect you have come a long way in that time.

What skills have you enhanced since becoming a parent?

> **What new skills have you developed since becoming a parent?**

Becoming a parent is not just something to get through alongside working. To manage. Although I hope some of the tips and insights have helped. It is something that really develops you as a person. And adds to your CV/résumé in ways you may not have imagined. So, the next time the realities of being a working parent are testing you to your limits, try and remember how much you have grown and how much more valuable you are.

Key takeaways from this chapter

- Remember, there are lots of positives about becoming a parent that you bring to your role and team
- Some things you will just be even better at than before, others will be new skills you've developed and will transfer to your role that you may not have even thought about
- Time management, ability to focus, perspective and empathy are all very typical parent traits which have huge value in the workplace
- Reflect on what's changed for you and how much you've achieved during a period of huge change in your life
- Remind yourself of this the next time you are having a tough day

If you're supporting your partner/someone close to you

Try and help them see all the positives from their time on leave. And consider how you have developed too in this time, particularly if you're also a new parent. Do you recognize the traits we've identified in them or yourself?

If you're supporting someone in your team

Take a moment to reflect on the skills we've identified. Have you thought about them? Do you recognize these in them? Can you see how these have made a difference in their performance/way of working? Do you think they see the value? Can you share how you've seen these have a positive impact on their contribution, especially if you know – or suspect – they are struggling? But also if they're not? Positive feedback and recognition is always welcome, but perhaps even more so by a recent returner who's confidence may be lower than normal.

Reflections on Part 3

As we come to the end of Part 3, it's worth taking a moment to reflect on the challenges of returning to work. How are you feeling about your return? What else can you do to make this new phase as a working parent be the best it can be?

Exercise 9.2: What are your takeaways from Part 3?

What are your key outstanding concerns?	Who could help? What actions could you take?

Closing thoughts

As I said right at the beginning, I have written this book with the hope it will help those becoming working parents. And, in particular, those not lucky enough to have this kind of support provided to them by their employer.

I sincerely hope that was you. That you found it useful. Interesting. That it perhaps made you stop and think for a moment. Maybe even surprised you and opened your eyes to challenges or ways to overcome them that hadn't crossed your mind. Or at the very least, helped you organize your thoughts and feel much more confident about the way ahead.

If that is you, I have one last request to reiterate. Pay it forward. Connect with other working parents. You won't be the only one feeling the way you do. Share your learnings and experiences. Help your organization do more. And if you want any help with that, or would like to share your thoughts on the book, please get in touch. I'd love to hear from you.

Catherine Oliver
January 2024
catherine@bluebellpartnership.com

Notes

Introduction

1. Number of parents in employment in the UK – ONS stats show an increase in the proportion of mothers in employment, as well as showing the employment rate is higher for women with dependent children than those without
www.ons.gov.uk/employmentandlabourmarket/peopleinwork/employmentandemployeetypes/articles/familiesandthelabourmarketengland/2021

2. Number of parents in employment in OECD countries – OECD figures showing the increase in maternal employment rates from 64% in 2006 to 72% in 2021 (weighted average for 25 countries including the US, France, Germany, Spain and Israel)
www.oecd.org/els/family/LMF1_2_Maternal_Employment.pdf

3. Number of fathers in employment in the UK – ONS stats show the proportion of fathers with dependent children in employment rose from 89% in 2002 to 92% in 2021, as well as showing the employment rate is higher for men with dependent children than those without
www.ons.gov.uk/employmentandlabourmarket/peopleinwork/employmentandemployeetypes/articles/familiesandthelabourmarketengland/2021

Part 1: Before you go on leave

1. Length of leave taken in the USA. 'Average Paid Maternity Leave in the US [2023]: US Maternity Leave Statistics.' Zippia.com. 7 February 2023
www.zippia.com/advice/average-paid-maternity-leave/

2. Parental leave in Germany
www.destatis.de/EN/Themes/Labour/Labour-Market/Quality-Employment/Dimension3/3_9_PersonsParentalLeave.html

3. Global variations in support for new parents
   www.ilo.org/wcmsp5/groups/public/---dgreports/---gender/documents/
   publication/wcms_838655.pdf

4. Surrogacy – number of births 2020
   https://brilliantbeginnings.co.uk/wp-content/uploads/2020/06/
   Parliamentary-briefing-paper-2020.pdf

5. Breastfeeding breaks globally – included in a report 'Care at Work' from the
   International Labour Organisation (a UN agency)
   www.ilo.org/global/topics/care-economy/WCMS_838653/lang--en/index.
   htm

6. Returning to work while breastfeeding in the UK – great article offering
   advice from the charity, Working Families
   https://workingfamilies.org.uk/articles/returning-to-work-while-breastfeed-
   ing-a-guide-to-the-law

7. Discrimination – Equality & Human Rights Commission
   www.equalityhumanrights.com/en/our-work/news/three-four-working-
   mothers-say-they've-experienced-pregnancy-and-maternity

8. Returning part time for full-time pay – Vodafone
   https://careers.vodafone.com/uk/whats-in-it-for-you/
   diversity-and-inclusion/programmes-and-policies/

9. Formal organization ramp-up policies – Airbnb
   www.linkedin.com/pulse/how-airbnb-invests-working-parents-katherine-rob-
   inson-galossi/

10. Flexible return provisions – Belgium
    www.thevillage.be/expecting-baby-belgium/types-of-leave/parental-leave/

11. Flexible return provisions – Germany
    https://familienportal.de/familienportal/meta/languages/family-benefits/
    parental-allowance-141952

Part 2: While you're away on parental leave

1. Changing your return date – UK
   www.gov.uk/maternity-pay-leave/leave

2. UK flexible working request changes – Flexible working bill
   www.gov.uk/government/news/millions-to-benefit-from-new-flexible-work-
   ing-measures#

3. KIT days and SPLIT days entitlement – UK
   www.gov.uk/employee-rights-when-on-leave

4. Vacation and parental leave – Germany
   https://einfach-elterngeld.de/en/parental-leave/vacation-entitle-ment-and-parental-leave

5. Accrual of annual leave – UK
   www.gov.uk/holiday-entitlement-rights; https://maternityaction.org.uk/advice/discrimination-during-maternity-leave-and-on-return-to-work/

Part 3: Returning to work

1. Provisions to look after sick dependants – Germany
   www.bundesregierung.de/breg-de/themen/coronavirus/child-sick-pay-1889416

2. Provisions to look after sick dependants – Singapore
   www.mom.gov.sg/employment-practices/leave/childcare-leave

3. Provisions to look after sick dependants – Spain
   https://riskandcompliance.freshfields.com/post/102iil8/worklife-2-0-spain-finally-implements-the-work-life-balance-directive

Note: All weblinks were correct at the time of writing.

Glossary of key terminology

Please note: these definitions are intended to help you understand some of the terminology. They are shortened to give the headlines for this purpose. For full formal definitions please check official sources. Similarly, all provisions detailed below are UK specific and were correct at the time of writing to the best of my knowledge, but as mentioned at the beginning, they change all the time so please use the links in 'Resources and further reading' to check the latest legislation and – if you're outside the UK – what applies where you live.

Term	Meaning
Accrued annual leave	While you're on maternity, paternity, adoption or shared parental leave, you continue to accrue both statutory and contractual annual leave in the same way as if you had been at work.
Adoption leave	Adoption leave is a right for anyone either adopting a child or a parent having a child via a surrogate.
Emergency leave	You have a right to a reasonable amount of time off to deal with an emergency. In the UK, this may be paid, but your employer is not obliged to pay you. Examples of when you

might use this include if your child gets chickenpox and you need to make alternative childcare arrangements or if they have an accident. Outside of the UK it is sometimes a paid right.

Keeping in Touch (KIT) days	KIT days are designed to help you stay in touch with the organization while you're on leave by working up to 10 days. They are totally optional – both the employee and employer need to agree to them. (KIT days are also a provision in Australia.)
MAT B1	This form is provided by your doctor or midwife in the UK confirming pregnancy. It's needed to enable you to claim Statutory Maternity Pay or Maternity Allowance.
Maternity Allowance (MA)	Maternity Allowance is a payment you can get when you take time off to have a baby if, for example, you are not entitled to Statutory Maternity Pay or are self-employed.
Maternity leave	Describes time taken off when you are having a baby. In the UK, this is called Statutory Maternity Leave – see below.
Maternity Pay	See Statutory Maternity Pay and Maternity Allowance
Parental leave	Both parents have a right to take up to 18 weeks of unpaid leave for each child up to their 18th

birthday. The maximum you can take in one year is four weeks and it must be taken as whole weeks unless otherwise agreed with your employer, or your child is disabled. It is designed to be used to look after your child's welfare, for example, settling them into new childcare arrangements, looking at new schools, hospital appointments etc., and some parents use this to help cover school holidays.

Parental Order   This is unique to surrogacy – it is used to transfer legal rights of parenthood from the birth mother to the intended parents.

Paternity leave   Describes time taken off when you partner is having a baby, or you're adopting a child or having a baby through surrogacy, and you've decided your partner will be the primary carer. In the UK, this is called Statutory Paternity Leave – see below.

Paternity Pay   See Statutory Paternity Pay.

Prenatal appointments   In the absence of any complications, there are typically up to 10 prenatal appointments for a pregnant woman to check on the development of the baby and the mother's health. In the UK, there are usually two scans, which typically happen at about 12 and 20 weeks. When pregnant you have a right to paid time off for all these appointments. Your partner has the right to attend two prenatal appointments. This includes those adopting (once you have been matched) and those using a surrogate. Many organizations offer paid leave for this, but not all and it is not a right.

If all is going well, they can be a very special moment. You may get to hear your baby's heartbeat for the first time, and you get that scan picture.

Return date	You must give your employer eight weeks' notice if you wish to change the date of your return post-maternity leave. The minimum amount of leave you can take is two weeks after your baby is born (four weeks if you work in a factory).
Shared Parental Leave (SPL)	SPL allows you and your partner to share up to 50 weeks of leave (the birth mother must take the first two weeks of leave) and up to 37 weeks of pay between you. The partner must give up some of their maternity or adoption leave and you can choose to take the time in blocks (i.e. returning to work in the middle). You are also free to choose if you take the time together or separately. You need to give your employer eight weeks' notice of your intention to start SPL.
Shared Parental Leave in Touch (SPLIT) days	These are the equivalent to KIT days for those on Shared Parental Leave; however, you can take up to 20 days and these are in addition to KIT days, so in theory a mother who ends her maternity leave early to take up SPL could work up to 30 KIT/SPLIT days in total.

Solo parent	There are differing definitions out there for single parent and solo parent. I have used single parent as an umbrella term for anyone with primary responsibility for the upbringing of a child and is not living with a partner. I have used solo parent to differentiate those who have either chosen to solo parent (for example via donation) or have become one on the death or desertion of their partner, vs someone who shares custody with a partner they are separated from or divorced. In the same way as some people are childless by choice and others not, some people are solo parents by choice and others not, but they are still doing this entirely alone.
Start date	This is the date you can start your parental leave. If you're pregnant, you can choose to start this before your baby is born (a maximum of 11 weeks before) or you can start the day after your baby is born. This is an area of great variation globally, so if you're outside the UK check this particularly carefully.
Statutory Adoption Leave (SAL)	SAL is 52 weeks, made up of 26 weeks of 'Ordinary Adoption Leave' and 26 weeks of 'Additional Adoption Leave'. If you're adopting, leave can start when the child starts living with you (or up to 14 days before the expected placement date), OR when they are matched with you by a UK adoption agency OR when the child arrives in the UK or within 28 days of this (in the case of overseas adoptions).

If you're using a surrogate, leave can start the day the child is born or the day after.

Statutory Adoption Pay (SAP)	The same as SMP, but provided to those adopting and the primary carer.
Statutory Maternity Leave (SML)	SML is 52 weeks, made up of 26 weeks of 'Ordinary Maternity Leave' and 26 weeks of 'Additional Maternity Leave'. You do not have to take 52 weeks, but you must take two weeks' leave after your baby is born (or four weeks if you work in a factory)
Statutory Maternity Pay (SMP)	SMP is paid for up to 39 weeks. It is currently 90% of your average pay for the first six weeks and then a nominal amount for the next 33 weeks. You will receive this via your employer. If you get enhanced maternity pay from your employer, they typically top this up to 100% so you won't notice any difference, except potentially in the frequency of how you are paid – if you are normally paid on a monthly basis, many employers switch you to weekly during maternity leave to make this easier.
Statutory Paternity Leave	In the UK, you can take two weeks within the first 52 weeks after birth. These can be consecutive or in two separate week blocks. There are different rules for adoption (see link listed under 'Resources and further reading').

Statutory Paternity Pay	In the UK, paternity pay is currently only statutory or 90% of your average earnings, whichever is less – so not much. Unless of course your employer supplements this, which an increasing number do – and in many cases now for longer than two weeks.
Statutory Shared Parental Pay (ShPP)	ShPP is the same as SMP except that SMP is paid at 90% of earnings for the first six weeks (with no maximum) – meaning for most people it makes sense not to switch onto SPL until after that first six weeks of leave.
Tax-Free Childcare	This is a UK scheme that replaced 'childcare vouchers'. As one parent said, 'it's like a bank account'. You pay in money to a special account, the government tops it up and you use this to pay your childcare provider. See the link in the 'Resources and further reading' section for full details.

Resources and further reading

Handbook

You can find all of the exercises in the book in a downloadable handbook at www.workingparents-to-be.com/handbook or by using the QR code below. This also includes all the references below and live links which will save you re-typing them.

Global

The best global reference I have found is the International Labour Organization (ILO) report. The ILO is a UN agency based in Geneva. The report (2022) is c.400 pages long but includes at-a-glance tables which give you a really good overview of the provisions in 185 countries around the world, as of 2021. There is also an Executive Summary which shares the key findings.

- Overview and full report: www.ilo.org/global/topics/care-economy/WCMS_838653/lang--en/index.htm
- Executive summary: www.ilo.org/wcmsp5/groups/public/---dgreports/---gender/documents/publication/wcms_838655.pdf

By country/region

- **UK**
  - UK government
    - Overview of policies relating to childcare and parenting including maternity, paternity, adoption and surrogacy: www.gov.uk/browse/childcare-parenting
    - Overview of your rights on parental leave including KIT days, SPLIT days, and job protection: www.gov.uk/employee-rights-when-on-leave
    - Pregnant employee rights: www.gov.uk/working-when-pregnant-your-rights
    - Maternity leave and pay: www.gov.uk/maternity-pay-leave/pay
    - Paternity leave and pay: www.gov.uk/paternity-pay-leave
    - Emergency leave: www.gov.uk/time-off-for-dependants
    - Unpaid parental leave – the entitlement to time off in addition to maternity/paternity/adoption leave that is limited to four weeks per year: www.gov.uk/parental-leave/entitlement
    - Shared Parental Leave: www.gov.uk/shared-parental-leave-and-pay
  - General advice on parental leave
    - ACAS (Advisory, Conciliation and Arbitration Service) advice for parents – covering your rights both as an employee and employer: www.acas.org.uk/time-off-for-parents
    - Maternity Action – maternity rights charity who offer a free helpline: https://maternityaction.org.uk/#

- Pregnant Then Screwed – advice line for guidance on rights, flexible working requests and questions about maternity pay/leave: https://pregnantthenscrewed.com/your-rights/
- Working families – UK charity for working parents and carers – support for employees and employers and helpline: https://workingfamilies.org.uk

  - Specific advice
    - MAT B1 Forms – Bounty (UK parenting club): www.bounty.com/pregnancy-and-birth/preparing-for-your-new-arrival/matb1-form-the-lowdown
    - Childcare Options – National Childcare Trust (NCT): www.nct.org.uk/life-parent/work-and-childcare/childcare/childcare-options
    - Childcare costs using Tax-Free Childcare – Working Families: https://workingfamilies.org.uk/articles/tax-free-childcare
    - Adoption Leave – Working Families: https://workingfamilies.org.uk/articles/adoption-leave/
    - Pregnancy loss – Tommy's: www.tommys.org
    - Shared Parental Leave for adoption or surrogacy – Working Families: https://workingfamilies.org.uk/articles/shared-parental-leave-for-parents-using-adoption-or-surrogacy
    - Pre- and post-natal depression – Pandas – advice and helpline https://pandasfoundation.org.uk

- **EU**
  - Overview of rights of those living in the EU with links to country specific employee benefits: https://europa.eu/youreurope/business/human-resources/

working-hours-holiday-leave/parental-leave/
index_en.htm#

- **North America**
  - Canada
    - Government of Canada – overview of maternity
      and parental benefits: www.canada.ca/en/services/
      benefits/ei/ei-maternity-parental.html
  - USA
    - Family and Medical Leave Act – overview from the
      US Department of Labor: www.dol.gov/agencies/
      whd/fmla
    - This article shares a good summary of the current
      provisions in the US, and how they vary by the
      state you live in and your employer along with the
      rules around PTO and what happens in practice:
      www.babycenter.com/pregnancy/your-life/
      maternity-leave-the-basics_449#

- **APAC**
  - Australia
    - Australian government overview of parental leave,
      rights including KIT days: www.fairwork.gov.au/
      leave/maternity-and-parental-leave

  - Hong Kong
    - Hong Kong Labour Department list of FAQs relating
      to employment including maternity and paternity
      leave: www.labour.gov.hk/eng/faq/content.htm

  - Singapore
    - Singapore Government (Ministry of Manpower)
      overview of parental leave and how this varies

depending on whether you are a Singapore citizen or not: www.mom.gov.sg/employment-practices/leave

- New Zealand
  - Employment New Zealand government overview of parental leave: www.employment.govt.nz/leave-and-holidays/parental-leave/eligibility/

Acknowledgements

I think this is probably the hardest bit to write in the whole book. I am grateful to so many people for their support and help in writing this. It's been incredibly humbling and it's difficult to get across what it has meant to me. I'm also really worried I'm going to miss someone!

I want to start with my husband, Jo. Who didn't question for a moment when I first voiced the idea. Who has always completely believed I could do it and has fielded endless questions, read various drafts and sense checked things for me. From the bottom of my heart, thank you.

I also want to thank our daughter, Evie. When I first had the idea for this, back in the Christmas holidays of 2021, she was 10. As I get the final manuscript ready to hand over to my publishers, she's 12. It's taken nearly two years of squeezing in the time to do this. And in that time, she's become my number one supporter. She's often nudging me when we're with others: 'have you told them?'. I love you for that and for so much more than you'll probably ever know – at least until you become a parent yourself. And I really hope if (when!) you do that it will be normal – expected even – to get this kind of support.

To my parents, Geoff and Elsieanne Snowdon, thank you for always being there for me, full stop. Not everyone gets so lucky, and I am aware of this every day. And to my brother, Chris, thank you for your support and our Friday chats, they have come to mean a lot.

I am also very lucky to have such a supportive group of friends and contacts who have been, without exception, incredibly encouraging and many have shown a special interest. Going out of their way to check in regularly to see how it's going. Making introductions. Listening and helping work through the challenges of writing a book. Thank you. It has meant so very much. Writing is by its nature an individual endeavour but being able to share each step of the way has made it feel like a team effort.

This is especially true of one group in particular. Those who went a step further and gave up their time to read the first draft of the book for me and give me their honest feedback. Who have acted as a sounding board to bounce ideas off during the process. I can honestly say every single point was thought-provoking and incredibly helpful, and I think you'll all see a great many ideas I chose to take on… so it truly has been a team effort and, I hope you'll agree, all the better for it.

This group included some of my best friends in the world, Vicky Lea and Andrea Lees, as well as friends I've made through work – Abdul Mullick, Al Weddell, Jane Middleton, our old nanny – Laura Hall, experts in the field (and friends) – Ollie Black and Rachel Vecht, and even someone I have not yet met in person, another ex-Sky employee and author himself – Nick Poulton. You are all amazing people, and I will be forever grateful for your advice, support and encouragement.

Then there are those who let me grill them on specific queries. Again, many of whom I have not ever met in person. Special thanks to Tamara Kaye, John Robarts, Ollie Kearton-Sipek, Amy Woltemath, May Fairweather, Corinna Stefani, Aline Wallasch and Georgina Gustafsson.

Plus, the fellow authors, who shared their experiences and learning of publishing – Catherine Garrod, Joy Burnford, Helen Beedham, Beth Stallwood and Han-Son Lee in particular.

I also want to thank the original Parents@Sky team and our supporters. I wouldn't be where I am today and have written this if you hadn't shared the belief in that early vision, and more importantly stepped up to help make it happen. There are many names I could put on this list, but I especially want to call out Clare Coleman, Abdul Mullick (a wholly deserved second mention), Jennifer Bryant, Natasha Behrens, Nicola Gamble, Zoe Hewlett, Dominic Wilkins, Sarah Astbury, Susan Townsend, Lucy Cox, Nashreen Patel, Fraser Johnson, Will Richards, Janine La Rosa, Mike Siebert and Clare Scott, for their endless passion and commitment. And our champions in the wider business, Colin Jones, Chris Stylianou, Deborah Baker, Sophia Ahmad and Sophie Turner-Laing. You all made a huge difference.

And finally, but far from least, my publishing team, Alison Jones, Shell Cooper, Michelle Charman, Nim Moorthy and Helen Flitton in particular, who believed in this from our first conversation, pushed me with just the right level of challenge, and have been there throughout to answer what I'm sure at times have been frustrating questions from a first-time author! I have really appreciated you being there every step of the way.

About the author

Catherine Oliver is a Diversity and Inclusion Advisor and Founder of the Bluebell Partnership. She specializes in helping organizations from start-ups through to the largest listed companies overcome the challenges of supporting working parents and developing their gender balance and wider inclusion strategies. Catherine previously had a 20-year corporate career, during which she became a mum, and founded and ran Sky's parenting network, Parents@Sky, with the help of a team of passionate and dedicated volunteers. Within a few years, the network had more than 1,500 members and a programme of activity including regular workshops, webinars, events and an online forum. Catherine went on to co-found Sky's award-winning Women in Leadership initiative, all of this alongside her 'day job' in the Strategy team. Additionally, she is a regular speaker at industry events.

A beach lover at heart, Catherine now lives on the south coast of England with her husband and daughter. Her other interests include travel (especially family road trips), learning the piano and dog walks on the beach.

A word about the Bluebell Partnership

The Bluebell Partnership (www.bluebellpartnership.com) was founded with the vision of creating a world of work where working parents and women in leadership can reach their full potential. Where flexibility is the norm – whether you have children or not. Where it's as commonplace to find a man taking parental leave on the arrival of a child as it is a woman. Where becoming a parent or being a woman in leadership is universally recognized for the value that can bring to an organization.

It has grown from there into an organization working with clients to help them develop and implement their wider inclusion strategies to help all employees reach their full potential in the workplace, whatever their background, personal circumstances and beliefs.

Clients range from start-ups through to the largest listed companies, across a wide variety of sectors from construction and leisure to property and professional services. Every engagement is tailored accordingly, but they all have one thing in common – they're not box ticking. They're trying to make a difference, to change how their organizations work for the better.

Find out more at www.bluebellpartnership.com or by emailing Catherine/connecting with her on LinkedIn.

catherine@bluebellpartnership.com
https://www.linkedin.com/in/catherineoliver/

Index